Acclaim f(

Raising Healthy Kids in an

David Altshuler's *Raising Healthy Kids in an* .... is so funny and entertaining that it's easy to overlook its usefulness—sort of like a snack that's so tasty you forget it's also good for you. The short essays he's collected here are meant to be reassuring yet also to challenge us to keep our parenting priorities straight. They're likely to provoke thought and conversation about how we act with—and think about—our kids. And did I mention they're also really funny?"

-Alfie Kohn
Author of *Unconditional Parenting* and *Punished by Rewards*

The personal and professional experience David brings to parenting both as a parent and as an educational consultant who has listened to and helped thousands of families is unmatched. David has a remarkable talent of weaving together stories and experiences and making us all think differently about our kids and ourselves. His insight, humor, and wisdom come shining through in these pages.

-Jeffrey Brain, MA, CTS, CEP.
Dean of Admissions, Allynwood Academy, Hancock, NY

As a child and adolescent psychiatrist and psychotherapist, I know the value of spending time listening to my patients and their parents in order to understand them and be as helpful as possible. I also know the value of working collaboratively with trusted colleagues in order to best help a family in crisis. Over the years, I have worked closely with David Altshuler as he has helped children and families. I know first-hand that he spends countless hours advising, supporting, and caring for them. His words of wisdom in this witty and entertaining book are but a small reflection of the valuable work he does.

-Sara K. Dann, M.D.

I have been reading David Altshuler's blogs on parenting and education for some time. Their arrival in my inbox are a highlight of my week. They are consistently interesting, thought-provoking, well-written, funny, and, if I dare use the word, wise. He is a treasure. How wonderful to now have a collection of them for review and continued reflection. You will find getting to know his mind a continuing treat, as I have.

-Jon Reider
San Francisco University High School

"Love the kids you get and you'll get the kids you love." That's David's seemingly simple aphorism. But there's much in the world and within ourselves which makes it difficult to follow. In these compassionate and humorous essays, David suggests that by knowing our children and tending to our relationship with them, we will be guided to what is best for them. Gently provocative, slightly subversive, and always sympathetic, David's writings help us to remember what is most important in raising our children.

-Douglas S. Feltman, M.D.

I have had the benefit of working with David Altshuler in attempts to ameliorate the mental health dynamics of many a family. In reading his book, his experience and expertise come across on every page. The chapters are written in an inviting fashion with vignettes, where embedded themes and principles seep past the individual defenses of the reader. Clinically minded information is presented skillfully and accessibly to the full-spectrum of readership. Not only is there a great amount of knowledge and wisdom for any parent, the presentation of said knowledge and wisdom keep the reader engaged through wit, drama, consternation about what "other 'bad" parents do, and, as noted above, clear themes and principles to address in each reader's parenting. Good on-ya David.

-Mayer Jeppson, Ph.D., Clinical Psychologist
Therapist, Second Nature Wilderness Program

Can anything new really be added to the conversation about how to parent our children? If you think not, then you have not read this remarkable book. It comes from a unique prospective and through countless conversations with parents and kids. It emerges from a father, educational consultant, and now published author who has a unique blend of insight, humor, and wisdom to share all gathered from the struggles of thousands of parents. It is woven together with love and wisdom and you will undoubtedly find new understanding and help in your own journey.

-Marsha Cohen, L.C.S.W.

David has a firm hold, not only on solid parenting principles, but also on the idea that presenting and teaching principles is important and meaningful in the lives of parents and families. Through short and entertaining snippets, penetrating and grounding truths are offered. I find this volume to be not only deeply insightful, but broadly so, having applications across all areas where one person might have meaningful influence on another.

-Shayne Gallagher
Executive Director, WinGate Wilderness Therapy

David's work with families and his advice and intervention have proven to be clinically sound and reflect a valuable common sense knowledge as to necessary directions of life. His work continues to reflect that of a true professional coupled with the delicate touch of a man who knows and cares. His compilation of work in this book is a tasteful blend of real problems, life experiences and clinical suggestions that have practical application. I find reading them to be entertaining and, more importantly, clinically helpful. I recommend reading David's work as either a supplement to professionals or as a self-help to raising children in today's world for families.

-Larry W. Carter, M.H.A.
Executive Director, Logan River Academy

Raising Healthy Kids
in an Unhealthy World

David Altshuler, M.S.

Langley Press

All inquiries should be addressed to:
David Altshuler
4520 SW 62 Avenue
Miami, FL 33155

www.DavidAltshuler.com
David@Altshulerfamily.com

ISBN-13: 978-0615797892 Langley Press

ISBN-10: 061579789X

Edited by Emily Cava Northrop
ECNorthrop@gmail.com

Cover design by Taylor Davis
TaetaeLovesArt@att.net

To my family, good story tellers all

Table of Contents

vi

Preface

For the past 30 years, I have had the rare privilege of listening to families tell the stories of their children.

In my admissions counseling practice—helping families choose and apply to college—families typically tell me of students who are having some trouble negotiating the "slings and arrows" of low processing speed, low self-esteem, or low expectations that are sabotaging their future. It is a difficult culture in which to bring up healthy children and even the most well-meaning of families can have a hard time avoiding the pitfalls of high school.

In my troubled teens practice, I listen to families whose kids are—for want of a more clinical term—a mess. Angry, anxious, and depressed, these kids are typically oppositional and defiant, as disrespectful as they are lost. I help these families find wilderness therapy and residential treatment facilities so that they can begin to heal. Some of these families have made obviously ridiculous choices—smoking pot with their kids, for example. For other families, it is hard for me to point a finger and feel superior. I would have made the same parenting decisions that they did. I am not at all sure why their children turned out to be so lost and unhappy.

With all my clients—from those who are heading to appropriate colleges to those who are one more DUI away from suffering long-lasting negative consequences—I think about what their families might have done differently.

Again, I don't pretend to have all the answers. It's easier to say what doesn't work than what does.

***

It has often been remarked that we are at war.

Those of us who hope to bring up healthy kids are under an unrelenting attack by unseen forces that want to harm our children. Ubiquitous process addictions—cigarettes, alcohol, marijuana, prescription pain killers, gambling, Internet pornography—join a culture in which poor parenting decisions are everywhere. Mean girls, bullies, imperfect educational institutions, underpaid teachers, and neighbors with ridiculous values assail us. Eating disorders, self-harm, and oppositionality, unheard of half a century ago, are now concerns in every community.

We stand here with our limited resources—our good judgment, our sense of how healthy families function, our longing for simpler times—trying to drive back a tide of heavily armed, well financed opponents. Cigarette companies, for example, claim that they provide a product for those who have already chosen to smoke. But if your kids want to buy cigarettes, no one from corporate will fly down to your local market to try to talk them out of it. Proponents of legalized marijuana suggest that marijuana is less addictive than nicotine or alcohol. (That's your best hold—that marijuana is less addictive than nicotine and alcohol, substances that kill hundreds of thousands of people every year in this country alone? Perhaps being shot with a rifle is preferable to being killed with a flame thrower, but that's a poor argument for standing in front of a rifle.)

What I'm hoping to offer here are reinforcements, affirmations if you will, to help you get through these tough times and bring up healthy kids. I invite you to stand with me. Just as alcoholics in recovery swear by the meetings they attend, just as many runners exercise in a group, just as dieters share recipes and ideas, those of us who want to bring up healthy kids need to support one another.

I don't pretend that there are easy answers. I don't ask you to rely on bromides that cannot possibly be helpful: "it was easier to bring up healthy kids generations ago;" "everything would be fine if both parents didn't have to work outside the home." This battle to keep our children safe is fought every day in every home.

The irony is that a warlike mentality isn't helpful. It's true that kids need to avoid addiction and stupidity. But kids also need to feel that their homes are safe. Parents who are strident or paranoid are less likely to make their kids feel safe than parents who are calm and authoritative. We need calm homes, homes where kids can make mistakes and learn from overcoming failure. Does this sound like an impossible challenge? How can kids learn from failure in a world where it is easy to get left behind where a single poor decision can have long term negative consequences?

It is my fervent wish that the following gentle suggestions may offer specific advice as well as hope.

Introduction

A buddy of mine had his first child last year. Lloyd was an older dad getting started and, like expectant parents through the ages, he had some concerns. He wanted to get it right, to provide love for his child and to help her grow up healthy and strong, independent and compassionate. He wanted her to be successful and accomplished, but he wanted her, above all else, to know she was loved. He had read a number of books on parenting, but didn't think the information was helpful or applicable. He said the advice was either too generic "Don't drop your baby" or too specific "If your sick baby doesn't respond to this antibiotic, try *this one*".

"What do I do, David?" he asked. "You're the expert. You go to all the conferences, you read books on parenting, you have four kids, and you've been giving advice to families for decades. What do I do?"

I closed my eyes, lifted my hands, waved them around, and pretended to take a hesitant step as if visually impaired.

"Follow me," I said.

***

Stated another way, I am not at all sure that the following essays will be helpful to you. My insights and gentle suggestions are culled from talking to thousands of families over the past 30 plus years and then following through to see how things are going down the road. I don't pretend that there's any science involved here. There's no control group of families who didn't follow my advice. And the families with whom I work—typically upper middle class and educated—are hardly representative of the population of this country, never mind the rest of the world. Just the same, I like to think that I have been helpful to some families. If my advice also seems too vague at times and too specific at others, I guess you could call Lloyd.

***

As any parent who has drawn breath in 2013 will attest, these are tough times to bring up healthy kids. The richest country on Planet Earth is also fraught with the most peril for children: marijuana and oxycodone are available at every high school; every convenience store carries incipient addictions—to tobacco, to alcohol, and to gambling. I recently asked a 16-

year-old girl in my office to guess how many boys in her tenth grade had never seen Internet pornography. She rolled her eyes as if I had asked her how many of her classmates had never eaten a French fry.

Hopefully, you will find the suggestions in the essays that follow not only generically useful ("Your kids shouldn't smoke pot"), but also utilitarian ("Here's how to improve the odds that they won't").

Here is a book about how to raise healthy, happy, content children—what Maslow might call kids on the way to being "self-actualized" adults. I hope you'll enjoy these essays and that they will be useful to you. And that you'll let me know if the suggestions are helpful to you in raising healthy children. If you'd like to join the conversation, I would love to hear from you.

I can be reached at David@Altshulerfamily.com or DavidAltshuler.com

An insidious attack on our ability to bring up healthy kids is the relentless call for information about them as if each child were starring in a well-publicized reality show. Our kids need to know they can share their grades and scores with their parents without that information showing up on social media sites.

Perhaps the gentle sarcasm of this essay will help encourage you to keep your children's private information private.

Privacy

"What did your daughter get on her math test?"
"Where is she applying to college?"
"What did she get on her SATs?"

These are the thoughtful, endearing questions that concerned parents ask one another in the parking lot as they wait to pick up their 11th graders after school. In our community, all the families care deeply about one another's health and well-being. The paradigm in our high schools is one of cooperation rather than competition. All the parents want what is best not only for their own children, but also for the children of their neighbors. Students good-heartedly help one another prepare for exams. Every high grade is a victory not just for the child who received it, but also for every other student in the class. After all, every child can achieve top grades; every child can get top SAT scores; every child can go to a top college.

What's wrong with this picture? Nothing much—other than it is complete and utter malarkey, a total fabrication. Not a word of the above has any validity in my neighborhood. I'm guessing your community is the same. Here's how it goes in the real world:

1) Students are trained to be brutally competitive. Susie won't help Buffy study chemistry because both girls are close to being in the top ten percent of students in their class. If Susie helps Buffy, then Buffy may be more eligible for scholarships and college acceptances.

2) Counselors post the names of where kids have been admitted to college. Big bulletin boards—or even worse, the school newspaper—proclaim not only where your child applied, but also where she is going to matriculate.

Abigail Van Buren-Princeton University
Maria Teresa Ortega-Miami Dade College

Why not just print the tax returns of both parents?

Abigail Van Buren's dad: Piles of money.
Maria Teresa Ortega's father: Not so much.

3) It's an arithmetic fact that not all children can graduate at the top of their class. By definition, only ten students in a hundred are in the top ten percent.

If you believe—as I do—that the choice of college is about the match between student and school, then you may wish to instruct your children to keep their SAT scores and their college lists private.

Here's why: A public humiliation is much more painful than a private one. If the only people who know where your son is applying to college are you and your spouse, then the thin envelope in April can be forgotten in 20 minutes. If, on the other hand, everyone in the school is buzzing "Did you hear? Anthony was rejected at Cornell!" then the sting of rejection can last months or longer.

Imagine how horrific it would be if a dinner guest in your home sat down and, in between the soup and the salad courses, asked you: "Say, nice house ya got here. How much did you pay for it, anyway?" Or imagine this conversation: "Yeah, my wife ain't making too much progress with them SSRIs, so we're going to go with an atypical anti-psychotic. I hope she don't gain too much more weight." The boor would never be invited back. Yet, these same people think it's okay to interrogate your children about private information.

Where your kids are applying to college and what they got on their SATs are no one's business. Their teachers don't need to know; your friends don't need to know; your colleagues at work don't need to know. And the parents of your children's friends at school certainly don't need to know. If you wouldn't tell a casual acquaintance the dollar amount of a bonus you received at work, why would you disclose personal information about your son's scores or college list?

This advice applies whether your child would be an appropriate match at a "top" school or at the local community college. Wouldn't it be nice to communicate to our children that we value them for who they are rather than for what they do? Wouldn't we like our children to know that we love them wherever they apply, wherever they are admitted?

When an adult asks your child a question about private information, have your child respond, "Oh, my dad says I'm not allowed to talk about where I'm applying to college. I'm sorry, but he says that's a family matter." Your daughter will have more respect in the community for valuing family and privacy, not less.

Privacy allows your children to benefit from knowing they are loved for who they are rather than for where they are admitted. Our schools will benefit from being places where students can study together more and envy one another less. Our communities will benefit in that they will be less obviously competitive places.

If intrusive parents persist and ask again what your daughter got on her SATs, then she has my permission to respond as follows: "'What did I get on my SATs?' Mustard. It's disgusting and it won't come off."

If annoying parents still won't take the hint, then it's time for nuclear weapons. When these boorish folks ask again, "Where are you applying to college?" your daughter should respond, "Are we sleeping together?"

When the interrogators respond with an embarrassed, "No!" then your daughter can go on to say, "Then we'll have to talk about something less personal."

When is "good enough" good enough? When do we communicate to our children that we are satisfied that they have done the best they could and that we value them for who they are—not for a particular result?

I Just Read About a Man

"Mom? It's me, Joel. Yes, everything's fine. The kids are great. They're looking forward to seeing you when you come up next month. What's that? Yes, my practice is fine. Thanks for asking. Removed three gall bladders on Wednesday. What? No, arthroscopic. It's called arthroscopic surgery. Yes, I think all the patients were covered by insurance. Silvie? No, I haven't spoken to my sister this week. I was away. Where? Sailing. You know we do the Mackinaw Island race ever year.

"This year was really something, Mom. That's what I wanted to tell you about. The weather on Lake Michigan was bad. Worst this century, they said. There was this squall that came out of nowhere, 40 mile per hour winds, four-foot seas. The race organizers were talking about calling off the race, but at the last minute they said we could go. What's that? No, it's not dangerous—we have all kinds of electronics—but it was scary. Two of my grad students were below decks throwing up. The lake was that rough. I was at the tiller for almost the whole race, close to 40 hours. About a third of the boats turned back. We heard that one of the boats had to be towed back to the marina. That's how bad the conditions were.

"Anyway what I wanted to tell you, you know how I've been doing this race every year, every year since I got out of med school? Well this year, after 23 years of doing this race? This year we won, Mom. How about that? Four-foot seas, 40 mile per hour winds, and we won.

"What's that? What did you say? You just read in the paper about a man who crossed the Atlantic in an 18-foot boat?"

The above story is true. I can't tell you how I know that it's true; you'll just have to take my word for it. The next story may be apocryphal, or it may be true. Unlike Joel in the anecdote above, Bernard Lown, the subject of the following vignette, is not a relative of mine. (Oh, darn, there I've gone and disclosed how I know the sailing story is true.)

In 1985, the Nobel Peace Prize was awarded to a group called the International Physicians for the Prevention of Nuclear War. The cofounder of the group, Bernard Lown, a world-renowned cardiologist, accepted the award on behalf of I.P.P.N.W. Watching her son ascend the dais in Switzerland, Dr. Lown's mother turned to her companion and, sighing deeply, said, "I had always hoped he'd win it for medicine."

Did the doctors in these stories achieve so much because their mothers had expectations that were so high? Or were these doctors dissatisfied that they were never able to achieve the approval they may have sought? If you're never good enough, if your best doesn't cut it, if there's always a higher mountain, then what's the point?

Haile Gebrselassie ran the Berlin Marathon in two hours, three minutes, and 59 seconds. This is the fastest time ever recorded. Of the seven billion people on the Planet Earth, no one has ever run that distance that fast. Of all the people who have ever lived, Gebrselassie is the fastest at 26.2 miles. In 2008,

18

he broke his own record in the marathon by 27 seconds. (He also has back-to-back Olympic gold medals in the 10,000 meters and over two dozen world records in distance events.)

I want to try to put this achievement in context. There are about 105 quarter miles in the marathon. It may seem a silly way to look at it, but 105 times a quarter mile equals about 26.2 miles. A quarter mile is the distance once around the standard track at your high school. Unless you are a trained athlete, unless you are much younger than I, there is no possibility of your running one lap—much less 105 laps—at Gebrselassie's speed. You or I couldn't run one lap in 71 seconds. Gebrselassie ran the first quarter mile in 71 seconds. Then he ran 104 more quarter miles in 71 seconds. You or I could have taken a taxi for the first 26 miles of the race, jumped out of the cab fresh as the proverbial daisy—and still lost. By a lot.

So here's Gebrselassie on the podium, receiving his award and being interviewed by journalists. Do the journalists ask him how it feels to have slaughtered the world record for the marathon distance? Do they ask him how his family back in Ethiopia feels about his stunning achievement? Do they ask him how he feels about another world record, his 27th? No, no, and no. The first question that journalists ask—journalists who couldn't run all the way across the parking lot to their cars without getting winded—is whether or not Gebrselassie thinks a sub-two-hour marathon is possible.

"I just read about a man who crossed the Atlantic in an 18-foot boat."

"I'd always hoped he'd win it for medicine."

"Do you think a sub two-hour marathon is possible?"

At some point "good enough" has got to be good enough. I'm going to be satisfied that my kids are doing the best they can. When it comes to grades, test scores, and especially college admissions, I'm going to be thoroughly satisfied and grateful when my students are admitted to good enough schools—whether or not Joel's mother, Bernard Lown's mother, or a group of random journalists have anything helpful to say about those schools.

"College is a match to be made, not a game to be won" is not only the most cogent advice about the admissions process, but also a powerful insight into how to bring up healthy kids. Before parents can love their kids for who they are, it's helpful to know who the children are. The mom in this essay knows who she wants her son to be—not who he actually is.

Mean Colonel Mustard

Why did Colonel Mustard kill Mr. Body in the Billiard Room with the Revolver?

As difficult as it may be to get a valid psychological profile of a one-inch tall, yellow bit of smoothed wood, I'm going to make the following inference: there was money involved. "Follow the money" is a good place to start when solving any crime.

In my line of work, college admissions counseling, "follow the feeling" is a good place to start when unraveling a family's motivation. To help a student make the right match, good counselors listen. After listening to the student, we also listen to the moms:

"Percival is very bright. He needs to go to a top school."

"Tell me more. What are his interests?"

"He has mostly As with some Bs and a few Cs."

"What is he passionate about?"

"He has As in Art and Weight Lifting."

"What makes him smile?"

"He has Bs in English and History."

"What does he feel is important?"

"He has Cs in math and science. But that's because his teachers don't remind him to do his homework. He should be in advanced classes, but the school counselor doesn't like him."

"How does he spend his time when he's not in school?"

"He should have done better on his SATs, but he didn't prepare and the conditions at the testing center were unacceptable."

"Where does he see himself in five years?"

"He's very bright."

"Is there anything else you'd like to tell me?"

"Yes. I already told you: He needs to go to a top school."

No, actually, he doesn't. He'll be slaughtered. He'll be unhappy and overwhelmed. He'll be outmatched and stressed out. He'll develop concomitant miseries—alcohol abuse if he's lucky, substance abuse if he's not.

21

I've been helping "top" students find themselves at top colleges for generations now. The profiles of these kids are remarkably similar: the toughest academic course load their high school has to offer; norm-referenced test scores well into the 90th percentile; leadership positions in meaningful, consistent extra-curriculars; and a work ethic that just won't quit. Percival won't do well in that rarefied atmosphere; he won't be able to breathe.

I'm very fond of Randy Starks, a Defensive End for the Miami Dolphins. He impresses me as a hard-working player and a decent guy off the field. But if we line up opposite one another across the line of scrimmage, it's going to be bad for my 56-year-old, 175 pound self.

Consider Gary, a solid B student with low processing speed and some other mild learning differences. With the help of his counselor, he has developed a list of colleges that would give him the support he needs and allow him to succeed both in the classroom and out. His mom's response that "no one at my country club has ever heard of any of these colleges" suggests that Gary's mom is looking out for her own interests more than for those of her son.

What is mom's agenda? It doesn't take much of an extrapolation to suggest what Gary's mom might be thinking about. Surely she wants what is best for her son. She may want Gary to be the kind of student who can go to a "top" college and succeed. Absent Gary being that kind of kid, mom may be hoping that Gary can appear to be that kind of kid. Again, I can suit up in orange and blue and try to block Randy Starks, but at 6' 3" and just over 300 pounds, he doesn't have a lot to worry about.

The lesson bears repeating: college admissions is a match to be made, not a game to be won.

Loving parents need to follow their feelings, gain insight into their motivations, and ultimately look out for what is in their children's interests. That way we help to ensure that the kids end up at the right places.

How do we help our kids grow up to KNOW that they're capable? Not by TELLING them that they are.

Dumb or Easy Versus Smart or Tough

My students, when telling me about classes in which they've done well, frequently say, "But that class was easy." Interestingly, more young women than young men suggest that they've done well academically only because their classes weren't that challenging. I don't think these 11th grade girls are being falsely modest. I think they have internalized the message that they only do well in classes that aren't that difficult.

Which is a losing proposition.

Everyone has problems they can solve and problems they can't. Of the thousands of high school students whom I have helped choose and apply to college, each and every one of them knew her ABCs, for example. None of them, on the other hand, could relate the four fundamental forces of the universe—the strong and weak nuclear forces, the electromagnetic force, and gravity—into one grand unified theory. (And just so you know, Einstein spent the better part of 30 years trying to figure this out without success. Apparently, it's something of a tough problem.)

So there you are: problems you can do—remembering that "elemeno" is four letters, not one—and problems that you can't do—come up with a Grand Unified Field Theory.

Now, why can you do the problems that you can do and why can't you do the problems that you can't do? Here you have to make what's called an "attribution." You can either attribute your success to yourself (I did the problem, I'm smart) or to something other than yourself (I couldn't do the problem, must have been a tough problem.)

Of course, it can go the other way too: You can attribute your failure to yourself (I can't do the problem, I'm dumb) and your success to the problem (I did the problem, it must have been easy.)

If your daughter thinks she's dumb, she's more likely to give up. If she thinks the only problems she can do are the easy ones, she won't try the more challenging ones. After all, there's nothing she can do.

On the other hand, if your daughter believes herself to be a capable problem solver, she'll be less likely to give up. The problems don't matter; she's the one who matters. Her success depends on herself, not on what the problem is.

When my kids get out of bed in the morning, I'm hoping that they don't believe that they're either dumb or that they're just getting easy problems. I'd like for them to think that they're smart and that the problems they can't do are hard. That way they're more likely to do their best, not give up, and learn a lot.

And don't bother just telling your kids that they're smart. Telling kids they're smart and capable and hardworking doesn't do anything for them. Sure, telling them they're smart is better than saying, "We only had you to save the marriage," but let's face it: you lied about the Tooth Fairy. Why wouldn't you lie about whether or not your kids are smart? Especially when it's clear to an impartial observer that you're invested in whether or not they are?

24

How do we help our daughters believe that they're capable? I don't know that I have definitive answers, but we'll kick around some ideas in the rest of the book.

With all that's written about WHY it's bad for your kids to let your divorce snowball out of control, there should be more information about HOW the situation can get so bad so fast. This article will also offer some incontrovertible advice for how to avoid the downward spiral of escalating fighting that is so detrimental to your children.

Dollar Auction

"The Dollar Auction Game: A Paradox in Noncooperative Behavior and Escalation" was published in the *Journal of Conflict Resolution* in March of 1971. Martin Shubik is the author. Here's how it works: the auctioneer says, "I'm going to give a dollar to the highest bidder, just like a regular auction. The only difference is that both the highest bidder (like any regular auction) and the second highest bidder (unlike a regular auction) have to pay the auctioneer the value of their bid."

Mr. Smith offers an initial bid of a nickel. This bid certainly seems reasonable. Who wouldn't want to get a dollar for five cents? And, according to the rules of the Dollar Auction, if no one else bids, Mr. Smith will indeed get a dollar for a nickel. Not a bad deal in these tough economic times.

Ms. Jones, however, bids a dime, reasoning as follows: I can get a dollar for ten cents. That's a good deal. I'll have to pay a dime and Mr. Smith will have to pay a nickel. But I'll get a dollar for my dime and he'll get nothing for his nickel.

(For the sake of simplicity, I will limit the explanation to just Mr. Smith and Ms. Jones. The argument doesn't change with more people.)

Mr. Smith is now in a tricky spot; if he remains quiet, he loses a nickel. Ms. Jones will get the dollar, paying only a dime, and he will get nothing for his nickel. Any rational person in Mr. Smith's place would bid 15 cents. Mr. Smith will still get 85 cents profit. And he certainly doesn't want to get nothing in return for his nickel. So Mr. Smith bids 15 cents.

But Ms. Jones now speaks up. She bids 20 cents. If she doesn't bid again, she will lose her dime. By bidding 20 cents, she will earn 80 cents if Mr. Smith doesn't bid again.

But of course, Mr. Smith does bid again. He has to. Otherwise he'll lose the amount of his previous bids. Similarly, Ms. Jones has to keep bidding.

Consider their reasoning as the value of the bids approaches a dollar: Ms. Jones has bid 95 cents. Mr. Smith bids a dollar. That's right. He bids a dollar to win a dollar. What choice does he have? If he doesn't bid, he loses his 90 cents and Ms. Jones wins the dollar and gets a profit of five cents.

So what will Ms. Jones do? She will do what any rational person would do. She can't lose her 95 cents and get nothing in return. She must keep bidding. She must bid $1.05. She has to bid more than a dollar to win a dollar.

Mr. Smith has to bid more than $1.05. Otherwise he'll lose his dollar and get nothing in return. He bids $1.10. Surely any reasonable person would agree it's better to pay $1.10 for a dollar than to lose $1.00 and get nothing. Losing a dime isn't as bad as losing a dollar.

Except of course that now Ms. Jones has to bid $1.15 by the same reasoning. She bids $1.15 to win the dollar.

Both Mr. Smith and Ms. Jones must now continue to bid amounts well in excess of the dollar. There is no point at which it makes sense to stop bidding. When Mr. Smith bids $4.00 to preserve his $3.90, Ms. Jones will bid $4.15 so she doesn't have to pay $4.05 and get nothing.

I'd like to write more about the dollar auction, but I'm too busy thinking about another situation. Tell me if you think the people involved in the following real life scenario could learn anything from the dollar action: These folks are getting a divorce. Coincidentally enough, Ms. Jones, the mom, kept her maiden name when she married Mr. Smith. One recent evening, Mr. Smith said he didn't feel like doing the dishes. Ms. Jones said she didn't love Mr. Smith. Mr. Smith said he had never loved Ms. Jones. Ms. Jones threw some of Mr. Smith's clothes out into the street. Mr. Smith froze the assets in Ms. Jones's bank account. Ms. Jones had an affair. Mr. Smith hired an attorney. Ms. Jones hired a forensic accountant. Mr. Smith accused Ms. Jones of giving their adolescent children drugs and alcohol. Ms. Jones accused Mr. Smith of being inappropriate with their daughter. Mr. Smith took Ms. Jones's name off the emergency contact card for their children at school. Ms. Jones refused to allow Mr. Smith to see the children last weekend when it was his turn for visitation. Mr. Smith told the family mediator that Ms. Jones is unfit to be a mother. Ms. Jones told the judge in family court that Mr. Smith is actually an alien from another galaxy.

Just kidding. Of course, I'm exaggerating. Ms. Jones would never go before a judge in family court and say that her husband, the father of her children, was an alien from another galaxy. What she said was that her husband was an alien from another solar system.

In any case, extra credit for any gentle reader who can solve the following problem: Given the rules of the dollar auction as described above, what is the only way to win?

Spoiler alert: The answer is in the next paragraph. If you would enjoy thinking about how to WIN the dollar auction before being told, STOP READING NOW.

The only way to WIN the dollar auction is not to play. If you bid any amount—even a nickel—you will be swept downward into a game that cannot be won. Similarly, if you must get divorced, DO NOT engage. If you have your children's best interests at heart, give in. Let your irrational, offensive, over-reaching, idiot of an ex have more than a 50 percent share. That's an expensive proposition, I know. But the alternative—psychically-damaged children who absorb their parents' rancor—is infinitely more expensive.

The only way to win is not to play.

Helping our children be appreciative can best be effected by modeling satisfaction in our own lives. Helping our children avoid dissatisfaction in their lives can best be effected by allowing them to make their own way, letting them fight their own battles.

Holiday Gifts

As a grandmother enjoys a sunny day at the beach with her five-year-old grandson, the sky darkens and an enormous wave comes out of nowhere, washing the child out to sea. Hysterical with fear, the grandmother frantically shouts to the lifeguard who is already sprinting toward the ocean. Fighting the chaotic waves, the lifeguard reaches the drowning child. After a heroic struggle, the lifeguard returns the child, unharmed, to the shore. The child picks up a plastic shovel and continues playing. As the lifeguard vomits seawater and lies on the beach gasping for air, the grandmother shakes her fist and shouts at him: "He had a hat!"

Many college admissions counselors to whom I have told that joke over the years have nodded sagely. They say, "Yeah, I know that family." Then they tell a story of their own. Here are a few of my favorites:

1) A student is given a new Lexus for her 16th birthday. Does she say, "Mom, Dad, you will never regret your generosity"? Does she say, "I'm going to wash this car every week and increase my hours at my part-time job so I can pay for all the gas and part of the insurance. I'm going to take my little brother to school and you can count of me for grocery shopping and other errands"? No. Instead she breaks down in tears and opines, "I was hoping for a BMW!"

2) A concerned mom comes to see her son's counselor at the school. "You just don't understand," she says. "My son is the second-best trumpet player in the school. If only the band teacher would spend more time with him, give him private instruction, help him after school, he would be the first chair." (Mom's statement may make some sense and evoke some sympathy until the gentle reader considers that the current first chair trumpet would then be second.)

3) "My child's life is ruined," Mom says to the high school admissions counselor in April. "He studied obsessively all through high school. He focused on his classwork, never wasted time helping his classmates (And why should he? They're all applying to the same top colleges). He had SATs in the top two percent of the nation." Mom pauses to press a tissue to her eyes. "But he was rejected at Dartmouth."

"Has he been admitted to any other colleges?" the counselor inquires gently.

"Yes. He'll have to choose between Middlebury, Davidson, Amherst, Williams, Haverford, Northwestern, and Wesleyan." Mom, untouched by irony, continues, "But he really wanted to go to Dartmouth."

What do all these hysterical piranhas have in common? What mistake are they all making?

1) Competition is a worthwhile paradigm in the NFL—less so in a high school math class. Children who concentrate on who is doing better than they are focus less on what they are learning. Just like a man who loves his job will never work a day in his life, a child who loves to learn will read and study

on her own.

2) We want to communicate to our kids that we care about them for who they are, not for what they do. Somebody has to be second chair trumpet. Unless your child is the next Leonard Bernstein, leave him alone.

3) I've been advising families about choosing and applying to college for over 25 years now. I'm working with the children of the children whom I counseled in the early 1980s. The following scenario never happens. Never.

A student who goes to Williams rather than Dartmouth ends up drinking wine in the gutter rather than getting an MD/PhD and living a happy, contented life.

That's right. Never.

Next time you consider haranguing your child's college admissions professional, take ten seconds to look at the world from their point of view: her yearly salary is less than the cost of a year of private college. And she's thrilled that your son has the opportunity to go to Williams—Williams being clearly distinguishable from the Bataan Death March.

"I wanted the BMW, not the Lexus."
"He should be first chair trumpet."
"He wanted Dartmouth rather than Williams."

"He had a hat."

Modeling inappropriate behavior increases anxiety in children applying to college. Helping your kids cheat and teaching your children that cheating helps are both ways to make a stressful process even more unbearable. Worse, by cheating, you communicate to your kids that the world is an unsafe place and that they are not okay just as they are. Do you truly want to convey that you would love your children more if they were performing at a higher level in the classroom?

Ethics

A student is caught texting during an exam. She is getting answers from her phone, a blatant violation of the honor code at her high school. The teacher looks at the student's phone. Who is on the other side of the conversation? Who is supplying the answers to the test? Are the answers coming from another student with poor ethics? No. The answers are being sent to the phone from the student's mom.

At another high school, a student turns in a paper. The teacher runs all papers through Turnitin, an online program that checks papers for academic integrity. (While teachers boast that they're not playing gotcha, there are those of us who argue that there is indeed something to be said for playing gotcha.) The paper is plagiarized, purchased from a website. The student's defense when confronted? "I didn't buy this paper." Well then, who did? Who purchased the stolen paper? Who paid for the plagiarized assignment?

Wait for it: the student's father purchased the paper and gave it to his son.

A student with impeccable (in retrospect, "improbable") credentials is accepted as a transfer to Harvard. He has 1600 boards and more AP courses than anyone in the history of the applicant pool. His recommendations are glowing—incandescent, really. Except of course, his entire file is a complete and utter fabrication. He faked the whole package.

Now, no matter how thin you make the pancakes, they always have two sides. Still, it is hard to imagine the contrasting view, the circumstances that would allow a mother to reasonably believe that she was acting in her daughter's interest by helping her cheat during an exam. It is hard to articulate the argument that the father could make as to why he purchased a paper for his son.

Surely, no reasonable parent would stand up as being in favor of cheating and plagiarizing. These examples are as egregious as they are deplorable, contrary to everything good educators stand for, that good parents believe, that good students talk about. Surely nothing comparable happens on a daily basis in admissions. Surely admissions is only about honorable people trying to select a well-rounded class from among many qualified applicants. Surely there are no prevarications, exaggerations, or outright lies. (And no, I will not stop calling you "Shirley.")

Is admissions always ethical? You be the judge. Here's what goes on in my world:

1) Fast Aps. The "Office of Enrollment Management"—known, in the late Pleistocene, as "The Office of Undergraduate Admissions"—sends "Apply Now!" emails to students in selected zip codes. "Fast aps" are, as the name implies, easy to fill out; many do not even require an essay. If your child

34

receives an email that begins "Apply Now!" wouldn't you infer that your child's chances of being admitted to that school are good? If you believe that your daughter was singled out for strong academic credentials and that the college will admit her, you could well be mistaken. The reason colleges send "Apply Now!" emails is that they want to increase the number of applicants. The reason that colleges send "Apply Now!" emails to your child is because you live in the right zip code—a zip code with high property values.

2) Financial Aid. "We guarantee to meet the demonstrated financial need of all our applicants." Pants on fire. There are maybe 20 schools who are well-endowed enough (read: "have enough money") to meet the demonstrated financial need of all applicants. Yet I have been told that "we meet the demonstrated financial need of all applicants" endlessly. I have visited over 200 college campuses and met with admissions personnel at most of them. If I had a nickel for every time I've heard that a college "meets the demonstrated need of all its applicants," my children would no longer qualify for need-based aid.

3) Dishonest Counselors. "I'll get you in." Counselors, both public and private, intimate, suggest, hint, imply, and sometimes just come right on out and say it explicitly: "I know someone, I'll get you in." Oh, and here's my favorite scam from a recent headline: "Give me money and I'll tell you how to dress for the interview." Give me money and I'll tell you how to dress for the interview? I'll tell you how to dress for the interview right here: don't show up naked. The interview itself has little influence on admissions decisions. How a student dresses for the interview? Even less. Yet some counselor had the unmitigated temerity to charge thousands of dollars for advice about how to dress for an admissions interview. "I'm seventeen years old and—dahling—I just haven't a thing to wear to my college interview."

Why do interviewers take photographs of students? Because they don't want to admit kids with acne? Wrong. Interviewers take photographs so that they have some hope—however small—that they'll be able to remember who the heck they interviewed at ten a.m. Tuesday by the time they've interviewed a dozen other kids by three p.m. Thursday. No admissions interviewer remembers what a kid wore to the meeting.

Here is the real role of the ethical counselor: to assuage anxiety about the admissions process, to dispel misconceptions about the admissions process, to help a student find her proper match. Gaming the system or giving the appearance of conveying an unfair advantage are both, well, unethical.

It's easier to fawn over the good old days that it was to actually live in them. There was nothing romantic about wondering whether or not there would be enough money to buy food for the kids on a given day. Life was hardly idyllic in this country during the depression, but there were a few advantages over 2013: at least you knew who the enemies were—privation and hunger— rather than the more ambiguous threats to our families today. There are lessons for how to raise our children today in the families of generations ago.

The Enemy

My dad was born in Philadelphia in 1924. At home. Delivering babies at hospitals was a new concept and didn't cater to poor families of new immigrants. When my dad was a few months shy of his sixth birthday, his father—after whom I am named—was murdered. Apparently my grandfather was something of a small-time criminal during prohibition. It wasn't until I was an adult that I put together all that had happened to my grandmother—my dad's mom—in late 1929. Her husband and sole economic support was killed while driving a beer truck. A month later, the stock market crashed leaving most families in dire financial circumstances. My grandmother, like so many families, had nothing—no safety net, no social services, nothing. With only an elementary school education and no training in any skill other than sewing, my grandmother went to work selling aprons door to door. Even by the low standards of the depression, this was a low-paying, lousy job. I asked my dad about how his mom had managed.

"Yeah, we had a bad year," he said.

There was talk of sending the children—my dad, age six, and my aunt, age four—off to a state facility, but my grandmother couldn't do it. Instead she moved in with relatives. There were 11 people in three rooms, the bathroom down the hall shared with even more families.

For his ninth birthday, my dad received an expensive sweater from a relative. His mom "bought" the sweater from him for a dollar. Then she sold the sweater to buy food for the family. Can you imagine the humiliation of having to steal a birthday gift from your young son in order to afford food?

There's nothing extraordinary about the extraordinary hardships my family faced. Compared to many, they had it easy. Yes, as a teenager my dad worked 40 hours a week while going to school, but at least he had a job. Yes, my grandmother had to steal a birthday gift from her son, but at least there were groceries as a result. Yes, my dad was drafted and trained as a ball turret gunner, but WWII ended before he was scheduled to go overseas. It could have been worse. Other families endured much more.

Let's leave my dad in the early 1950s—he's looking forward to meeting my mom and having a couple of kids—and consider an episode of "Leave it to Beaver," one of the first sit-coms. From 1957 to 1963, Beaver's mom, who didn't work outside the home, served meals with fresh vegetables. She wore pearls and immaculately-pressed dresses to dinner. Here's a typical plotline: Beaver and his friends break a neighbor's window with an errant baseball. They agree to lie about the incident to avoid punishment but subsequently come clean and fess up to dad who is stern but understanding. The boys get a job bagging groceries to earn money to reimburse the woman whose window they broke.

"Beaver" has been criticized for not being representative of our country at the time. There were no characters of color. Indeed, I don't remember a single Black, Hispanic, or Asian face from any episode. But whether or not the show was indicative of our culture, consider what was unspoken: Boys with crew cuts sat down to dinner with their families and had conversations about morals, social conventions, and proper behavior.

A generation later, "Married with Children" was a popular sit-com. A loveless marriage, children obsessed with hook-ups lacking emotional intimacy merge with countless references to all things sexual. "Married with Children" is about as far from "Leave it to Beaver" as Botticelli's "Madonna and Child" is from Madonna.

Let's go back to my dad in the early 50s. Thanks to the GI Bill, he's almost through with law school by now. My dad and his family—the whole generation—knew who the enemies were: job loss, hunger, cold, and starvation in the cities. Hunger, hail stones, crop failure, cattle disease, cold, and privation in the country. The enemy was outside the home. As Mary Pipher points out in the best book I've read about families, the enemy today is seeping in under the door. *In the Shelter of Each Other* talks about how young people are faced with choices unheard of 50 years ago. Addictions of all kinds are attacking families: Internet pornography, drugs and alcohol, gambling, and sex. To this list of threats are added the ubiquitous screens— movie, television, and computer—modeling disrespectful behavior in adolescents. That which destroys families is inside the home.

"All my friends are allowed to drink."
"All my friends drive their cars past curfew."
"All my friends have girls sleep over."
"Their parents don't mind, why should you?"

Ignoring for the moment whether or not these first three allegations are accurate, the parents of the adolescent in this example are already at war. They have to have a conversation that would have been unheard of half a century ago.

My special-needs clients frequently tell their parents, "It's all your fault, you're so stupid, I hope you die. Why don't you just shut the f*** up, you f***ing bitch?"

I feel sorry for these kids and am eager to help them get the treatment they need. Can you imagine a child in the 1950s addressing his parents this way?

Our families are under attack by a toxic culture intent on selling them bad products and worse values. Fifteen-year-olds today have to decide on a daily basis whether or not to become sexually active, to play violent video games, to smoke pot, to watch pornography on the Internet, to go on-line and gamble.

What's the answer? We no longer have to protect our children from privation and cold. The enemy today is in our homes rather than in the elements. I would suggest that we inoculate our kids against the "everyone is doing that" argument. Try to make your family the rock on which your morals are based. "Here's how we do things in our family" can be the start of many a conversation. "In our family, we only watch TV on the weekends;" "In our family, we don't play video games;" "In our family, children are not allowed to smoke marijuana or drink alcohol;" "In our family, we have dinner together every night." (Pearls and long dresses are, of course, optional.)

Don't you wish your kids only had to decide whether or not to fess up to having broken a neighbor's window?

*The following article was written in response to an excerpt of Amy Chua's
book Battle Hymn of the Tiger Mother, which was originally published in
the New York Times on January 19, 2011. As always, I hope my gentle,
over-the-top sarcasm instructs rather than offends.*

BOBO

Recently another parenting article found its way into print by the next in a
line of namby-pamby, touchy-feely, peace, love, ten-speed, hearts and
flowers, knitting, granola, Whimpasaurus moms. Amy Chua argues for no
sleepovers. Of course sensible parents who want what is best for their
children do not allow sleepovers. Sleepovers are filled with other foods, other
ideas and—here's the worst of it—other people's children. No sleepovers
may be a good place to start, but to ensure that your child ends up as
Number One, no sleep is the only way to go.

In my recently published best seller, *Parent Ineffectiveness Training (PIT)*, I make a point based on my sophisticated and deep understanding of the base ten number system. Unlike other "foreign" number systems with who knows how many symbols for the number one, in America, there is only one Number One. When your child is sleeping, my child is practicing the bouzouki and that's all there is to it. My house, my rules, baby.

"But my hands are bleeding and I want to sleep," my child frequently signs. (Too young for actual speech, our daughter was taught to sign just after she finished her APGAR prep seminar. Needless to say, she got a perfect ten.) "Oh, your hands are bleeding and you want to sleep?" I respond. "Go back to practicing. Your mother and I only had you to save the marriage."

There can only be one Number One and that's going to be MY CHILD. Your child can be Number Two—and I mean that in every sense of the phrase. Of all the symphonies in all the orchestras in all the cities in the country there can only be one first first violinist and that's going to be MY CHILD. Your child doesn't matter. So go ahead and let her take time off for eating. What difference will it make subsequently when your child is drinking wine in the gutter and my child is the first chair bouzouki player at the world renowned BOBO? (That's BOston Bouzouki Orchestra, if you didn't know.)

Don't believe me? Think that there have been other happy people in the world who weren't the product of two married professional parents, one of whom is Asian, living in New Haven? Van Gogh? Never played violin, didn't sell three paintings in his life, didn't amount to a hill of sunflower seeds. Throw out that baby, the bathwater, and the empty paint tubes. That Albert dude? Well known as a terrible violinist. Terrible. Other examples of developmentally-delayed failure children? I can't name them all. Everyone except my child.

"Love your child for who she is not for what she does"? What clap trap. Some years ago, the eldest of my 17 children (Free Parenting Tip: When family planning, focus on prime numbers) brought home a 96 on a math test. "It was the highest score in the class," she said proudly. "What's the matter, they don't give 100s in that class?" I responded before hitting her with the bouzouki. "Now drop and give me 20!"

All those developmentally-delayed children, the cognitively impaired, those with learning differences? Pish and tosh! They would all be Number One had they not been coddled. As many insightful educators will attest, there is no such thing as learning differences although there is such a thing as lazy children.

***

As always, here's the real deal for the chronically irony impaired: not all children can be Number One. By definition, only one child can be first chair, first in the class. If the only way your child is going to be happy is by being first, then there are going to be many disappointed children. If the only way mommy is going to be happy is if her child is number one, mommy might consider hopping in her Lexus for a trip to the hobby store.

We want our children to be content, fulfilled, self actualized. Success is great But I'd rather my child be a happy artist than a miserable attorney. Betting all your happiness on your child's success is a losing proposition. "If winning isn't everything, then why do they keep score?" Vince Lombardi said. But there can only be 11 Green Bay Packers on the field at a time. That not everyone can be Number One isn't a complex philosophical proposition; that not everyone can be Number One is an arithmetic fact.

Speaking of math, if having content children is the goal, then letting them find their own way has got to be part of the equation.

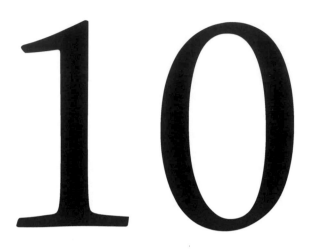

Here's another gently sarcastic piece about a father who can't understand why his son "refuses" to eat chocolate. Yet there are parents out there who, on a daily basis, deny that there are children who learn differently.

Chocolate

How many times have I told him to just have a Milky Way bar? Just one lousy candy bar. It's not like I'm asking for the world. Why won't my son just have some chocolate?

Yes, it's something of an emotionally-laden issue for me. I admit it. See, my father and I used to go out and have a chocolate shake. Or we'd go down to the Malt Shoppe and have some chocolate candy. But my son won't have any chocolate with me.

I've taken him to doctors. They keep talking about "diabetes." They say my son has "diabetes," whatever that is. These "doctors," these so called "experts," say that if my son eats chocolate he'll go into shock, have blurred vision, be fatigued, and have to go to the bathroom all the time. What hooey! If he would just try harder, he wouldn't have any of those symptoms.

All he does is complain. He says that there really is such a thing as this "diabetes" nonsense, that it's real. He says that his pancreas doesn't produce enough insulin. What drivel.

If he would just try harder, he could eat chocolate. I know he could. I'm pretty sure he doesn't eat chocolate just to annoy me, because he knows how much it means to me.

On the other hand, maybe we did do something wrong; maybe it's something we did when he was younger. For example, my wife nursed; maybe she should have bottle-fed. We sent him to pre-school when he was three; maybe we should have waited until he was four. We were too permissive; maybe we should have been more strict. I think if we had bottle-fed, waited a year before starting him in pre-school, and were more strict, he would like chocolate.

We've been to every chocolate specialist in town. Dr. Hershey said that behavioral interventions would work, that we should take away our son's cell phone until he agreed not to go into shock when he eats chocolate. Then Dr. Cadbury said that three therapy sessions each week for our son to talk about his relationship with chocolate would be more productive. Dr. Ghirardelli said that the best solution would be to just forbid our son all other foods besides chocolate. "When he gets hungry enough, he'll eat chocolate," the doctor said.

I'm at my wits' end. Even if he won't eat chocolate with me, if at least I could know that he's eating chocolate with somebody else, I'd be okay with that. In any case, we clearly can't give up. Chocolate is important to our family, has been for generations. We'll keep trying until we get it right.

Before you suggest that this father be immediately commended to the Nobel Nominating Committee for "Fathers Who Don't Get it at All," two quick points: first, let's try to be sympathetic. Dad doesn't understand diabetes. He's never heard of it. Diabetes wasn't an issue when he was a kid, at least not in his family. He wants to have a good relationship with his son; he wants them to spend time together doing that which he and his father liked to do.

He's even willing to have his son eat chocolate with somebody else. Dad isn't a bad guy; he's just not educated. He doesn't know the existence of, let alone the meaning of, words like "pancreas" and "insulin."

Secondly, change "diabetes" in the paragraphs above to "learning differences" or "executive functioning issues" and the discussion strikes a lot closer to home: "Why isn't my son doing well in school? I always did well academically, as did my father before me. We've always been a successful family. Yet my son doesn't do homework and when he does, it's not done well. His handwriting is terrible. Why won't he do the assignments properly?" Then the recriminations start and the assigning of causes: "Maybe it's our fault that our son doesn't study effectively and efficiently. Maybe the curriculum is too hard, too easy, too boring, not relevant. Maybe our parenting style is too strict, too lenient, too sarcastic, too turquoise."

Just as it's hard to imagine a kid not liking chocolate or a kid who goes into shock after eating chocolate, it's hard to imagine a kid who wants to do badly in school. Nobody ever woke up one morning and thought: "I have an idea. I'll lose my assignment pad and spend all of recess looking for it! That way my mom will yell at me, I won't be allowed to have dessert, and then I can go to bed early after a big fight. Plus I'll have the added joy of showing up in class tomorrow without my homework so that my teacher can yell at me in front of all my friends too!"

Kids with learning differences or kids with executive functioning issues (call executive functioning issues "attention deficits" if you like) don't want to have learning differences or executive functioning issues any more than a kid with diabetes wants to not be able to eat chocolate. And just as a kid with diabetes needs to acknowledge, embrace, and articulate what her diet should be in order to be healthy, a kid with learning differences or executive functioning issues needs to be able to acknowledge, embrace, and articulate what's going on is his head so that he can learn effectively.

Parents and educators can help these kids by being sensitive to their learning styles and understanding that almost all kids want to learn, want to fit it, want to do well.

The alternative assumption—that kids are refusing to eat chocolate just to annoy you—leads to some odd conclusions.

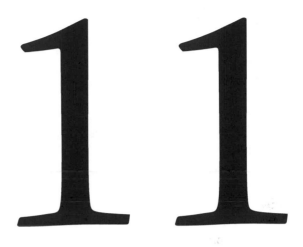

Listen to this mom before judging her. What could she have done differently? What would you have done in her situation? Would you agree that there is enough blame to go around?

Where Did I Go Wrong?

I'm at my wits' end about my son. I can't even begin to tell you how bad it's gotten. He's 17 now, but I've been having trouble with Andres since the day he turned two-years-old. He just won't do anything I tell him, even the simplest little suggestions, even when they're clearly for his own good. I might as well be yelling at the ocean.

Even when he was little he was out of control. I would pick him up from aftercare and he'd be bouncing off the walls when we got home. I would want to have a glass of wine and take a bath, but he'd be all over the place. I have to work; his deadbeat father sends me enough child support to pay for about one new sneaker a year. I used to leave the house at six a.m. to drop him at the program that takes care of the kids before school. When I get home—after being yelled at half the day by my psychotic, idiot of a boss—I need some peace and quiet; I need to regroup. So I did everything you can think of, everything anybody recommended to keep the kid quiet: I bought videos for the TV, I bought computer games, I bought about a hundred Kiddie Cable channels. But the child would not leave me alone or stop moving for five minutes. You can't cook dinner, never mind relax after a hard day, with a kid who's climbing all over the furniture and trying to grab on to the ceiling fan.

School was a nightmare too. I kept getting calls from teachers; he wasn't doing homework. I tried everything to get him to comply. Homework is important. If kids don't have the discipline to do homework at age six, how are they going to have the discipline to make contributions to their retirement accounts when they are 40?

And he wasn't paying attention in class the teachers said, wouldn't focus on the lessons, wasn't learning as quickly as the rest of the kids.

I took him to the pediatrician. Thank goodness I have good health insurance from work. The doctor said that if my son wasn't paying attention in school then he must have attention deficits. I asked the doctor if he needed to see my son or ask him any questions and he said no, that it wouldn't be necessary. He prescribed a psycho-stimulant—I forget the name. Adderall maybe. But it didn't help. My son was still full of energy, running all around the house, wanting to play all the time, constantly asking me questions, annoying the heck out of me.

Somehow we got through elementary school. But in middle school things got even worse. Andres started moping around. All he wanted to do was skateboard. I didn't want him hanging around with those kids; where I live "skateboarder" is another word for "pothead." I didn't let him go out to the skate park. (Can you believe it? We don't have money in the city budget for proper police protection, but we have money to build half pipes.)

Andres acted more and more depressed, so I called the pediatrician. Again. The doctor gave me a prescription for an anti-depressant. I asked if I should bring Andres in so the doctor could see him, but the doctor said that an SSRI would be helpful. Andres didn't want to take the pills—he said they made his mouth dry and his head feel fuzzy—but what was I going to do?

The doctor said Andres might be bi-polar and that the pills could help. I looked up "SSRI", Selective Serotonin Reuptake Inhibitor, on the Internet. I didn't want Andres to be bi-polar.

But the pills didn't help. Andres still wasn't doing well in school. He still wasn't hanging out with the right kids. He was in tenth grade by now. I told him a hundred times: there are such nice children at the high school. There are kids involved in student council, kids working together on the yearbook, kids volunteering at Habitat for Humanity, great kids doing great things. But all he wanted to do was hang out with the skateboard crowd. And I know those kids were all smoking pot.

So I took Andres to a psychiatrist. The doctor was on my health plan, thank goodness. He could only see Andres for eight minutes. (I think if you're that busy, you must be a good doctor.) He prescribed an "atypical anti-psychotic"—Abilify, I think it was called. Again, Andres didn't want to take it, but I insisted. He was going down the wrong road. The only kids he wanted to be friends with were those pot-smoking, thuggy skateboard kids. And they were the only kids who wanted to be friends with him. The doctor and I both thought the medication would help him, but I don't think it did.

Now we're supposed to be choosing and applying to colleges. He doesn't have the grades to get into a good college and anyway he's not interested in going. Worse, the other day, I found pills in his room—Xanax. He says the pills don't belong to him, that he's holding them for a friend, but I don't believe him. Eighty pills? Why so many? Could he be selling them? If he's dealing drugs, I will be truly heart broken.

I feel terrible. I wish there were something more I could do or could have done when he was younger. I sacrificed everything for Andres. I never remarried. I never even dated much. I was working all the time just so we could live a halfway decent life. I'm even making okay money now. I feel like I've done everything, tried everything, and now I just don't know what to do.

***

It's easy to throw a stone at this parent, to give advice about what she did wrong. Clearly her child would have benefited from more time outdoors, a more developmentally-appropriate schedule, some time to relax and grow into the ability to make good decisions. Homework for first graders directly contradicts everything we know about how kids learn to love learning. It could also be argued that she was too controlling, telling Andres what to do rather than working with him to come up with a life that would make sense to him. A little human interaction, rather than all those TV, video games, and computer screens might have been helpful as well. And obviously, Andres wanted a peer group. All kids do. But no one in the group of "good kids"—the active and involved kids—would want to hang out with him. The "pothead" kids are more accepting. You don't need any social skills, you don't need any commitment, you don't need any abilities. You just need to be willing to smoke pot. Which is not a high barrier to cross.

The progression of prescribed "fix my kid" medications is as unfortunate as it is common: psycho-stimulants for attention, followed by SSRIs for depression, followed by atypical anti-psychotics and mood stabilizers. (Who wouldn't be energetic after being in school for ten hours at age six? The after school program at our neighborhood elementary has a curriculum of compliance—sit down and pick up a pencil—rather than one of discovery, joy, and age-appropriate running around.)

There's enough sadness here—overworked single mom, overburdened school, insensitive pediatrician, incompetent psychiatrist, inappropriate peer group—to go around.

Rather than pointing fingers and blaming this mom, here is some pointed, if difficult, advice. It's always easier to talk about what someone else did wrong than to make suggestions for what they might have done differently.

Leave the kid alone about homework when he's in first grade. Little ones develop a desire to read at different ages and a "one size fits all" approach isn't appropriate. Forcing children to do homework before they're ready always backfires.

Mom could have made a significant economic sacrifice to have been able to spend more time with Andres when he was little. The time will come soon enough when Andres will want to spend time with peers rather than mom. It's hard to know how a single mom without child support can make it in these tough economic times. But Andres has to be kept out of aftercare every day after school. Ten hours of sitting down is too much for six-year-olds. No wonder he was trying to jump on the ceiling fan when he got home.

50

The succession of drugs prescribed by pediatricians and psychiatrists who never even met the child is a travesty. You can't blame mom for trusting the professionals, but I would never recommend allowing a child to ingest such serious mind-altering pills without more information. What you don't take can't hurt you. In this case, the psycho-stimulants, SSRIs, and mood stabilizers were all contraindicated. Andres isn't a psychiatric kid; he just needed some time to play.

The TV shows, video games, social media, and computers all have to go. Of course Andres doesn't want to read or study. Why would he when the alternative is constant stimulation?

What's the prognosis for Andres and a million kids, now young adults, just like him? Not good. Without academic skills, without the motivation to work hard, without the experience of success in anything other than skateboarding and selling Xanax, the likelihood of a content and fulfilling life is small.

Again, more than enough blame to go around.

The following essay may seem odd in a book about advising parents how to bring up healthy kids. Long story short: we don't know everything there is about how to bring up content, fulfilled children. Obviously there are factors over which we have little control—developmental disabilities, accidents, and tragedies to name just a few—but the fact of the matter is that the "science" of parenting does not yet have all the answers. Optimistically, we can offer a "best practices model." Worst-case scenario, we are still stumbling along in the dark.

Fault Lines

Blaming gives me great comfort.

If Mickey Owen hadn't dropped the third strike in the fourth game of the 1941 World Series...

If I had bought AOL in 1992...

If I had sold AOL in 2000...

If Lee Harvey Oswald hadn't shot JFK in 1963...

And those Hatfields and McCoys. Don't even get me started about whose fault that was and what would have been different.

Would the Dodgers have gone on to beat the Yankees rather than having to wait until 1955? Would I be a wealthy man? Would the US have avoided the conflict in Southeast Asia? Would our country be stronger and happier?

It makes me happy to think of all these positive outcomes. It gives me a sense of righteous indignation when I hear about what the Republicans (or Democrats) have done (or haven't done.) If only our elected officials had the good sense to buy (or not buy), pass (or repeal) a law, address (or leave alone) this issue.

Parents get blamed as well for the poor behavior and poor performance of their children. Sometimes this paradigm makes perfect sense: a child who is up late at night may be tired and do poorly the next day in school; a child who is beaten will invariably learn violence; abused children almost never grow up to be healthy.

But sometimes the blame is harder to assign. "Refrigerator moms" were blamed for their children's withdrawn behavior in the 1950s. "Because you aren't warm and loving," they were told, "your children are autistic." Although there is still controversy about the causes of spectrum disorders, unloving parents is no longer a theory with any traction at all.

And what works with some children doesn't work with every child:

"We did everything the teachers, the counselors, the psychologists, and the psychiatrists told us. We set up behavioral contracts, we rewarded and punished, we read every book on parenting."

"We're simple people; we don't drink or smoke. We were loving, not abusive. We went to every soccer game, did what we thought was best. But our son hates us, hasn't spoken to us in years; we don't even know where he is."

"We have three other children, none of whom was ever a problem. The other three all went to college, lead happy and productive lives. But with our younger son, nothing worked. The more we tried, the worse he got. We got notes home from the teachers, we got advice from friends, we took him to every professional. He's 21 now, and he's a real mess."

"We were made to feel like it was our fault."

It's easy to throw stones at this family. It's fun to find fault: you were too strict; you were too lenient. You went to too many soccer games; you didn't go to enough soccer games. You shouldn't have made him play soccer; you should have made him play more sports. You should have hired a math tutor; you hired too many math tutors. You should have let him find his own way; you should have given him more direction. You should have given up after the first $50,000 spent on treatment; you should have spent another $100,000 to help your son."

The other side of this issue—parents who claim credit for their child's every accomplishment—burns me up. People frequently corner me in Publix (where, apparently, chatting is also a pleasure) and tell me their children's SAT scores. "Tabitha got a 1300," they intone. Then, in a conspiratorial whisper, they continue, "We read to her as a child."

If only good parenting were that simple. If only it were the case that by reading and loving, all our children would grow up to live contented and fulfilled lives. If only the direction of the causal arrow were that clear and straight.

I'm not making a case for nature over nurture. I'm just suggesting that our current models for how to bring up happy, healthy kids are way too simplistic and don't work for every child in every family. I'll let Will bring us home:

Yea, there thou makest me sad and makest me sin
In envy that my Lord Northumberland
Should be the father to so blest a son,
A son who is the theme of honour's tongue;
Amongst a grove, the very straightest plant;
Who is sweet Fortune's minion and her pride:
Whilst I, by looking on the praise of him,

54

See riot and dishonour stain the brow
Of my young Harry.
O that it could be proved
That some night-tripping fairy had exchanged
In cradle-clothes our children where they lay,
And call'd mine Percy, his Plantagenet!
Then would I have his Harry, and he mine.

In other words, because his son is drinking, whoring, and thieving, Henry IV wishes his enemy's kid were his.

In sum, here's what I've learned after 30 years of advising parents about how to educate their children:

Love the kids you get and you'll get the kids you love.

Take your kids to the woods or you'll end up paying someone else to take them.

When nothing is working, try something else.

13

Having admitted that we are a long way from knowing everything about how to bring up healthy kids, we do have good information about what is extremely unlikely to work: conditional love. Loving our children for what they do rather than for who they are never works. High expectations help children. Not accepting them even when they are doing what they can leads to tragedy.

The Scarlett Ibis School of Parenting

Tami still hadn't taken a step at 24 months. Because her mother carried her everywhere? Because her mother "enabled" Tami in her "addiction" to being enveloped in her mother's arms? "How will she learn to walk if you just carry her everywhere?" helpful strangers suggested. "Put the baby down and she'll walk."

No, she won't. Tami has some developmental delays including fairly severe cognitive impairments and an organic neuro-muscular problem. Her family's lovely pediatrician was able to pick up on the disabilities. Tami, now 13 with the intellectual capability of a five-year-old, loves to play dress up, goes to the bathroom by herself, goes to school, and walks beautifully on her own. Her parents adore her. They are okay with the fact that Tami will neither learn to play the violin nor get a PhD in philosophy from Princeton.

A gifted doctor was able to diagnose Tami's disabilities. But what if her differences were more subtle, harder to perceive? What if, oblivious to Tami's capability, her parents had screamed at her, threatened and punished, promised and rewarded, coerced and cajoled? What if they had been ashamed of their daughter's differences? "All the other children are taking their first steps at a year," they might have said. "We better put her down on the carpet. If she doesn't accept the responsibility of walking, then we'll just leave her there. We'll incentivize her. If she doesn't walk over here to the table then we just won't feed her. That way she'll learn to walk."

Before calling the Department of Health and Rehabilitative Services, consider just how many families inadvertently mistreat their children in exactly this way.

"He's bright; he just doesn't want to study."

"He chooses not to do his homework."

"He's not studying because he knows how much it annoys me when he gets bad grades."

Nah.

It's not about you. It seems like it's about you, but it's not. You love your kids so much and you want what's best for them, but their poor performance doesn't have anything to do with you. Their poor performance affects you. But it's not about you.

Kids want to do well. Here's why they don't:

1) They're distracted by screens. Many kids will eat potato chips rather than balanced, healthy meals if given a chance. Kids will play World of War Craft rather than read *The Hobbit, Sounder, A Wrinkle in Time*, or *Rabbit Hill.* Most kids will watch TV rather than learn spatial relations and engineering

by playing with Legos. The majority of adolescents would prefer to play "Shoot, Shoot, Shoot, Blood, Blood, Blood, Kill, Kill, Kill" rather than to learn fractions by baking cookies and selling lemonade. That's why screen time should be severely limited if not eliminated. Not only is what's happening on the screen damaging in itself, it's what the kids aren't doing when they're plugged in that is so harmful.

2) They have issues with drugs or alcohol.

Adolescent brains are still developing through age 25. Do the math.

3) The curriculum is mind-numbingly boring and meaningless. Imagine being asked to memorize the names of the 67 counties in Florida. That's what the eighth grade children in Miami, Florida were asked to do. Visualization imagery notwithstanding—"See the *Manatee* standing on the *Orange* next to the *Gulf* made out of *Clay*?"—could you force yourself to do something so, for want of a better word, stupid?

4) The students are lacking a skill—a skill understanding the likely result of their actions, a skill regarding keeping their emotions in check, a thinking skill, a time management skill—some kind of skill. For a more thorough and eloquent explanation, see Dr. Ross Greene's wonderful book, *Lost at School: Why Our Kids with Behavioral Challenges are Falling Through the Cracks and How We Can Help Them.*

The research is clear: in order to help our children develop to the highest and most appropriate level of academic achievement and contentment, yell at them until they achieve what you want them to do. Control their every thought and action. Force them to play the violin. Insist that they be first in their class. Be clear that you love them only for what they do, not for who they are.

Just kidding. The Scarlett Ibis School of Parenting is only even marginally appropriate with kids who have the horses to begin with. And even with super smart kids, The Scarlett Ibis School of Parenting produces high achievers as often as Harry Harlow produced happy monkeys. In my office, I seldom have to help parents make a choice between having high-achieving kids and having happy kids, but if I did, I know what I'd advise. Helping kids achieve the most they can given who they are is done by having high expectations and lots of unconditional positive regard. Stated another way,

58

even if you could make a silk purse out of a sow's ear, you'd still have one unhappy pig.

No adolescent ever woke up in the morning and said, "I have an idea! I'll do poorly in school so I can get negative attention. I'll be a pariah to my family, my teachers will be mean to me, and I'll get all kinds of detentions and other punishments! I'll get started by doing my homework in a thoughtful and complete manner and then deliberately leaving it on my desk.

The scenario above—a student willing and able to do homework and then refusing to turn in the assignment—is as unlikely as two-year-old Tami "choosing" not to walk.

Here's another cautionary tale of a well-meaning mother who got it completely and utterly wrong. Her heart is in the right place; her head, not so much. Before turning the page thinking, "What an idiot; everyone knows better," try to be sympathetic. There are thousands of moms in our city doing the same thing. Worse, maybe you and I are making similar mistakes with our kids—mistakes that seem obvious to everyone else. This mom did what she thought was right and the results are horrific.

Zen Screed

A handful of sand in a pile. Remove one grain of sand. The pile remains. Remove another grain. There is still a pile of sand. Remove another grain and another and another. At some point, there are just? a few grains of sand. When did the pile of sand become only a few grains?

All kids experiment with drugs and alcohol. I didn't want my 16-year-old daughter to be left out at parties, to be a social pariah. Of course, I allowed her to have a few beers, smoke some pot. Everybody at my high school did drugs and alcohol. There was nothing I could have done about it anyway. It's not like I approved, mind you.

Sure the police brought her home a few times, said they found cocaine and ecstasy in her car. But my daughter said it wasn't hers. And it's not like she was doing poorly in school or anything; her grades were fine. I told her that if she wanted to smoke pot that she should do it at home—where I knew she would be safe. "It's not you I don't trust," I told her. "It's them." But then the kids with whom she was hanging out started to look, well, stoned, even during the day. One kid in particular, I heard, was a mid-level drug dealer, stealing prescriptions and delivering oxycontin to families in our neighborhood. But my daughter said that wasn't true—that the rumors about the kid spread because other kids were jealous. About two years after I first suspected my daughter of doing drugs, her grades started to slip. I asked her if maybe she should cut down, but she said she had everything under control. Except the other day the police showed up again. This time they said my daughter was caught with thousands of dollars' worth of prescription medications, that it's a matter for the courts, and that she needs rehab.

I don't know what to do. I always told her: "If you're going to use drugs, just do them in moderation like I did."

***

Part One

At what point did this child cross over the imaginary line from substance abuser to addict to chemical dependent?

I am sensitive to the great number of my students who smoke pot—only occasionally!—and (seem to) suffer no ill effects. I know there are high functioning doctors, lawyers, and Indian chiefs who drink to excess. I've heard of butchers, bakers, and candlestick makers whose lives are full and meaningful even though they take prescription painkillers every day.

I chat with families all the time about the "risks and rewards" of turning a blind eye to their adolescents experimenting with drugs and alcohol. Here is a variant of a story that I hear frequently:

"Dr. Gropenheimer is now a respected heart surgeon in Philadelphia and he was a walking pharmaceutical company all through high school, college, med school, and residency. He was always so stoned, you could get high just by walking on the same campus."

Perhaps. But is this the way to bet?

The problem with the Dr. Gropenheimer story is that it ignores the denominator. Okay, skip the math word. The problem with the Dr. Gropenheimer story is that it doesn't include the cemetery. For every Dr. Gropenheimer, a successful heart surgeon in Philadelphia or elsewhere, there are a number of kids who never made it to med school, or out of high school for that matter.

Because they're dead.

The only way to ensure that your children do not become addicted to drugs is to see to it that they never start. Otherwise, the reward of the children being invited to parties doesn't outweigh the risk.

Simply stated: if you want the best chance of watching your children grow up healthy, of dancing at their weddings, of playing with your grandchildren*, do whatever you have to do to make sure that your kids don't get started with drugs and alcohol.

***

Part Two—Recipe for Rabbit Stew

Step One: Catch a rabbit.

Most families agree: it's easier to keep kids from starting to use drugs than to get them off drugs once they've started. Which brings us to the— admittedly—harder question of how to help keep our kids from starting.

There are few models in our culture of kids having fun sober and there are even fewer models in our culture of kids being physically intimate sober. What can families do to increase the odds that their kids will stay away from that first experience with marijuana?

62

My permissive families argue that the controlling families are too strict. "That's why the kids do drugs," they suggest. "Because they're not allowed to make any meaningful decisions."

My strict families argue that the kids of permissive parents are allowed too much latitude. "Of course those kids do drugs," the say. "Look at how their parents let them get away with anything."

I'm not sure that the relevant variable has to do with controlling families or permissive families. I would ask you to look instead at modeling—"Do as I say, not as I do" seldom works. And clarity of message is critical: are you a "zero-tolerance" household? Are you sure? Do your kids know that there's a zero tolerance for drug and alcohol use? How do you know?

I'm also concerned with the "everything is always going to be okay" message that many of my most loving families convey to their children. "Nothing will ever hurt," they exude. "And if it does there's a pill for that." I don't have any research to back up this idea, but I bet a kid who experiences a summer cold under medicated or has some trouble attending in school but isn't given a psycho-stimulant is more likely to avoid self-medicating years down the road.

Lastly, I'm a firm believer in the "pick 'em" school of parenting. Nobody ever died from leaving a sweaty tee shirt on the floor in his room. The "nobody ever died from..." construction can't be used in a conversation about drugs and alcohol. As parents, we need to help our kids distinguish between that which we believe strongly—zero tolerance—and that which we prefer—folded tee shirts.

* Are these examples—dancing at weddings, playing with grandchildren—deliberately manipulative, designed to pull at your heartstrings? Only if the manipulation works and I can help one child somewhere stay healthy.

15

Brains are different. As parents and teachers, we ignore this obvious fact at our peril. Of course, all children should be encouraged to work hard and to learn as much as they can about as many subjects as they can. But insisting that your child learn that which she cannot is a recipe for disaster. Not everyone can learn everything.

The Ballad of John and Yoko

My buddy, Pete, can play any song he's ever heard.

We call him the human jukebox. From "Little Old Lady from Pasadena" to "Lady Madonna," from "Maybelline" to "Layla," he knows them all. And not just 60s songs either. He knows every jazz song he's ever heard and every classical piece. Baroque? Romantic? Not a problem. Folk songs? Don't insult him. He's unstumpable.

What about a song he's never heard before? Play it for him. He'll listen to the first verse and then on the second verse, he'll play along with the chords. By the third verse, he plays along to the melody. Every note.

I play guitar too. Do you know what an emu is, that large ostrich-like bird? Imagine the sound of an emu choking on a trumpet. While being pushed down stairs. Inside a file cabinet. The sound of an emu choking on a trumpet while being pushed down stairs inside a file cabinet is preferable to the noise generated when I slam my leaden hands across my electric guitar strings.

Just the same, Pete will frequently condescend to play with me. We've been friends coming up on 40 years, after all. I'll play chords—I know several of them—and he'll play the melody or improvise. You know "The Ballad of John and Yoko"? We plug in two cables, crank up my amp all the way to eleven, and play as loudly as we can until someone—invariably a member of my immediate family—threatens to call the police.

"The Ballad of John and Yoko" has three chords—E, A, and B. Then at the end of the song, there's another chord, an E6. It took me some time to get the pinkie finger of my left hand to press down on the string to get that E6, and I was pretty pleased when I finally did. I'd been practicing for some time and I wanted to show off for my buddy. After all, just because he knows ten thousand songs doesn't mean I can't know ten songs. I played the E6 at the end and then, with a mischievous grin, asked my buddy for the name of the obscure chord. I was pretty sure that no one—certainly no one from the Planet Earth—could possibly know what chord that was.

"E6," Pete said.

How obvious was it to him that the chord was an E6 as opposed to, say, an E7 or an E9? Or an A6? I don't know. How obvious is it to you that the name of your first-born male child is Matthew, say, as opposed to Esmeralda?

Pete has "relative pitch," which means that if you tell him the name of one note, he can tell you any other note in comparison to it. He doesn't have "perfect pitch," which would allow him to be woken up in the middle of the night by a loud note and tell you the name of that note taken out of context.

Years ago, when Pete was performing at the university to earn a second graduate degree in guitar, I mentioned that his abilities—remembering any song he'd ever heard—seemed prodigious.

"A mere parlor trick," he assured me. "See that guy over there? He can listen to a chamber orchestra with four voices: two violins, a cello, and a viola."

"Big deal," I said. "I can listen to chamber music too."

"Yes," Pete went on. "But the next day can you write out the musical notation for all four instruments like he can?"

"No. Not so much," I agreed. "I'm lucky if I can remember where I parked my car."

What do these musicians and their uncanny abilities have to do with my usual topics of self-esteem and good parenting?

The first take away here is that there is always somebody better. Even if you are a human jukebox, you can feel good about your abilities or you can compare yourself to the guy who can write down every note of four instruments the day after the concert. Surely music is yet another example of an activity in which a practitioner should do the best he can and be content with the result.

And what about those of us who have iron ears and little musical aptitude whatsoever? After we've given it our best shot, should we be chastised and humiliated from one decade to the next? "David chooses not to advance to the next level," my music teacher might have written on my evaluation. "He *refuses* to remember the notes to every song he has ever heard."

I met this week with a lovely young man, an eighth grader who is doing poorly in school. Although Enrique loves to read—about Percy Jackson, Harry Potter, Lemony Snickett—he has trouble writing essays. He has "output failure." It's an especially tricky situation because he's so verbally adept. He communicates well, makes connections, and abstracts effectively, but he has terrible trouble getting the information out of his brain onto a piece of paper. His terrible handwriting affects his ability to do math as well: it takes him an age to write down one line of an equation and by the time he is three lines down the page, he can no longer read what he has written above. His "4" now looks like a "9." And taking notes? Fuhgedabout it.

When his teacher begins, "The seven causes of the French Revolution were..." his teacher has covered the first three reasons and is explaining the fourth one while Enrique is still arguing with his hand. "Make a capital 'F' for 'French,'" he says to his hand. "When I feel like it," his hand responds.

Because of his difference—his hand lags so far behind his brain—Enrique is at a disadvantage in the classroom. As you might imagine, his teachers are at a loss. So in their evaluations, they bludgeon him with the word "choice." "Enrique chooses not to do his best on classroom notes," they write. "Enrique chooses not to do a good job on his out–of-class essays."

Just like I "choose" to be unable to hear the difference between an E flat minor and a B flat minor chord. Just like I've "chosen" not to be able to memorize 10,000 songs.

What is the answer? What is to be done for those of us who learn differently? The same thing that we are doing, however slowly, for other underrepresented populations. Women were thrown away for generations. In the 90 years since earning the right to vote, they have made some progress. It is now time to allow our next under-represented population—those of us with learning differences—to shine in the many ways that we can, even if we don't have perfect pitch.

16

How hard is it to be Aaron Rodgers? How hard is it to be a high achieving student in small classes at a wonderful school?

Good Students

Good students are such a joy. I still remember my good students from the Carter Administration. Seriously. (Seriously, I remember my good students. I'm not certain they were involved in policy decisions in the late 70s.) Bright, eager, articulate, pleasant. They did homework, scored well on evaluations, contributed to class discussions. I never had to call their parents about their performance. These students enjoyed extra credit problems and worked hard on them. (Two thirds of two is what part of three?*)

Over the years I've kept up with many of these kids. The Census Bureau's assertions to the contrary notwithstanding, Miami is a small town: I run into my old students frequently. I love hearing about their successes and accomplishments, meeting their families, catching up on what they've been up to these past 30 years. It's great to hear about their graduate degrees and their startup companies. But I sometimes wonder—in spite of all the work—how hard it actually was.

Aaron Rodgers wasn't my student. (Born in 1983, Rodgers certainly could have been my student, but since he grew up in California rather than Miami, he wasn't.) I wonder how hard it is to be the best there is. Aaron Rodgers earns eight million dollars a year; I can't even guess how much money he gets to give a talk. He gets carried off the field after winning football games, and I suspect he has little trouble getting dates.

I'm not taking anything away from how hard Aaron works—training in the heat, playing in the cold, practicing twice a day, studying films, learning plays, traveling, playing in front of critical fans. Sports writers say he's the best there is.

But I still wonder how hard it is to be Aaron Rogers.

And I wonder how hard it is to be one of my high achieving high school students from a generation ago. They went to a school that, in today's dollars, costs $30,000/year. Some classes had as few as nine students, none had as many as 22 other kids. Teachers were uniformly excellent—highly educated, sympathetic, erudite. Their expectations were high, as was their regard for their charges—a recipe for good outcomes.

Not to take anything away from these great kids of whom I'm so fond, but what did I really contribute to their success? What did we as a faculty do to engender their achievement? What did the institution do to effect transformative positive change?

Maybe it would be more illustrative to talk about the kids who didn't make it at the highly competitive, college preparatory, elite school where I taught. At the end of every school year, we would meet as a faculty to discuss the few kids who had not been offered reenrollment contracts for the following fall:

"Melanie refuses to do her math homework."
"Russell won't pay attention in class."

Half a lifetime later, I wonder if maybe these kids had issues with "can't" rather than "won't." Of course, untreated, "won't" can take on a life of its own.

Why didn't Melanie do her homework? With the benefit of perfect hindsight, I'm guessing that she couldn't, not that she wouldn't. She didn't know the material; she had attention issues; she had problems writing; she was a slow processor.

Which is not to exempt these kids from personal responsibility. There may be legitimate excuses for not doing well on a math test, but there is no reason not to be a contributing member of your family. There is no gene that prevents a healthy kid from clearing the table and putting the plates in the dishwasher. There is no excuse for playing video games rather than bathing the dog. There is no reason to text your friends when you should be helping your dad in the yard.

My buddy Phil started exercising a couple years ago at age 60. He hates the gym—hates it—but attends religiously. Even though he knows better, he feels that he is not welcome in the workout room, that people are looking at him. But he keeps going.

When he first showed up, he couldn't run from his car to the door; now he can run a full mile without stopping. He has dropped 40 pounds; both his blood pressure and cholesterol are down. He's talking about signing up for a five kilometer run this year.

Couldn't it be argued that Phil needs our help and support to achieve his goals more than Aaron Rogers does? Shouldn't we as educators reach out to Melanie rather than focusing our attention on those natural high achievers?

Our whole educational culture impresses me as giving manicures to a few supermodels and refusing to offer a crust of bread to a stadium full of starving students.

* 4/9

We spend a lot of time yelling at our kids to make good choices, to stay sober, to choose the right friends. We spend less time helping them to do so.

Where Are the Sober Kids?

Kayla could hardly be described as a "bad" kid. Yes, she has shown poor judgment on a number of recent occasions. Yes, she skipped school and brought five friends home to drink beer in the middle of the day. Yes, her grades are below her ability and her motivation to do better in the classroom is modest. And yes, she did manage to have a run in with the police on the beach in San Diego over spring break because of an open container.

Okay, so Kayla isn't going to win an election for class president or homecoming queen any time soon. And she's not going to graduate from her California high school at the top of her class and matriculate at Stanford either. Indeed, she may not graduate from high school at all if her grades don't improve. She thinks her curriculum is boring and stupid. She can hardly be expected to do well in her algebra II class; she doesn't enjoy math and doesn't have a firm foundation in algebra I.

But she's not a bad kid. She's certainly not a psychiatric kid. She's not an acting-out kid. She doesn't cut herself, she doesn't have an eating disorder, she doesn't run away. She is respectful of her parents; she doesn't curse at them or threaten them. She helps out around the house. She drives close to an hour each weekend to visit her grandparents and take them food shopping.

In addition to being a gifted artist, Kayla is pleasant. She's helpful around the house, is responsible for the care and feeding of the family's cats. Her teachers like her well enough—although, of course, they too are disappointed that she's not working to her potential. And to be fair, her parents are at their wits' end. Kayla's two older brothers, both now in college, were much more serious about their studies.

Kayla's parents are considering some serious actions. They love Kayla and want what's best for her. Kayla's parents are both first-generation Americans and are the first members of their families to go to college. Kayla's parents are thinking about pulling Kayla out of school. They are thinking about "military school." They are talking about "boot camp." They've asked me about wilderness therapy.

Before intervening at this level, I thought we should look at local options. It's not like Kayla is a danger to herself or others. Of course, I'm vehemently opposed to alcohol for teenagers, but at least Kayla had never been behind the wheel of a car when she had been drinking. And she's smart enough not to drive with anyone who has been drinking. Again, I don't even know that she has ever been drunk.

Indeed, Kayla would be happy to hang out with some sober kids.

If she could find any at her high school.

Or anywhere in her community, for that matter. Because we've talked about options, Kayla and I. Endlessly. We have generated any number of ideas without much success. The options for Kayla are not stop drinking beer and go get a PhD in philosophy from Princeton or stop drinking beer so she can finish her training to be an astronaut. The alternatives for Kayla seem to be stop drinking beer and she'll end up with no friends.

What about the joining the Yearbook staff? What about getting involved with student government? What about options outside the high school? What about a great class at the San Diego Art Museum? What about athletics? There must be some sober kids somewhere. Southern California is a big place.

Kayla was respectful and thoughtful about each of these suggestions. Then she patiently explained how the kids involved in each and every one of these activities were also drinking beer. And worse.

The research of adolescent drinking is clear: kids who start drinking in high school are four times more likely to have serious alcohol issues as adults; teenage drinkers may lose up to ten percent of their brain power; adolescent drinkers are more likely to suffer from depression.

So my question for this essay is as follows: where are the sober kids in your community? Kayla—not her real name and she doesn't live in San Diego either—is mobile. Tell her where she can find some good friends who can get through a weekend sober and her family will seriously consider moving to that town.

18

You don't have to flip through too many channels before finding a great many folks who are willing to give you the benefit of their advice. Sometimes the agenda is clear, "Buy this product and send me some money." Sometimes the agenda is less so, "Listen to my political commentary and I'll be invited back on this TV show." There is a great deal of guidance about how to raise healthy kids. Much of it is benign, but some can be harmful.

Good Advice

A father and his son are preparing in the pre-dawn hours to travel to the market town, a full day's journey away through neighboring villages, across rolling hills and valleys. As the father finishes loading their donkey with the provisions needed for the day, he tells his son to get on and ride. His son demurs, and, out of respect for his dad, insists that his father be the one to rest on the donkey. "You brought me in to the world, my most blessed Father," he says. "I will not rest while you walk."

"You are my most beloved, son," replies the father. "Please ride. I am pleased to walk." After the son bestows many kind words of respect and affection for his father, they set off—the son riding, the father walking. Their journey progresses uneventfully as the sun rises over the countryside. They pass fields of wheat growing on both sides of the dirt road and watch as farmers toil in the early morning mist. Suddenly, one farmer throws down his threshing tool, hurriedly approaches the travelers, and addresses the son:

"Is this your father?" he asks.

"It is," the boy replies.

"And do you respect him?" continues the farmer.

"Above all men living," says the boy.

"Yet you allow him to walk on this sweltering day while you ride in comfort? The man who gave you life, you treat in this fashion?" The boy looks down in shame as the farmer continues, "It is he who should ride, young man, not you. He has worked hard his whole life; you are young and strong."

Without another word, the boy gets down off the donkey and helps his father get on. They travel in this way until the sun is high overhead, when another farmer in another town approaches them. "Hey, Old Man!" he shouts. "Is that your son?"

"It is," the father replies.

"And do you have affection for him?"

"He is the light of my eyes," the father agrees.

"Then why do you allow him to walk on this hot day while you ride and relax? He has his whole life ahead of him."

Silently, the father gets down from the donkey and helps his son get up. They continue traveling in this fashion until they come to yet another village where they are approached by yet another farmer. Without preamble, he addresses our travelers: "Is that your donkey?"

"It is," replies the farmer.

"And has that donkey worked hard for you for many years, carrying your burdens and helping you to plow your fields?"

"It has."

"Yet now you force this animal to carry you all day long in this dust and heat." The father and son cast their eyes downward. "Here is what you must do," continues the farmer. "You must carry the animal who has performed such good service for you all these years."

The father and son pick up the donkey and, carrying him, continue on their way.

They are approached by yet another farmer who tells them to sell their donkey and to buy tech stocks. They do as they are instructed. The time is early 2000. With the proceeds from the sale of their donkey, the father and son buy AOL, JDSU, Lucent, Nortel, I-Omega, and other companies with unprecedented price to earnings ratios. Within a few weeks, these stocks have lost 80% of their value. The father and son are now living in a trailer park on the edge of town. The father has high blood pressure, the son diabetes. They watch game shows on their 15-inch television and drink beer. They seldom speak.

***

Do you feel that you have been getting well meaning, but—for want of a better word, stupid—advice about your teenagers their whole lives? Do you feel that the people spewing this advice—the "parking lot mafia"—know nothing of you or your family? Do you feel that, whether or not you follow their advice, your path is still hot and dusty and that you are making slow progress if any?

For an out-of-control teen, have you been told, "You need to be more strict"? Have you also been told, "You need to be more lenient"? For a teen who is not working up to his capacity in school, have you been told, "Don't help him with his homework; he'll only become dependent and not know how to fulfill his responsibilities on his own"? Have you also been told, "Of course, you should help him with his homework; otherwise he won't feel loved"? For a teen with a substance abuse problem, have you been told, "Let him smoke pot at home; at least he'll be safe"? Have you also been told, "Don't allow him to smoke at all; force him to give up marijuana"?

Are you sitting down? Are you ready for the oddest question you've ever been asked in all your years of parenting?

What if it doesn't matter what you do? What if all these variables—strict versus lenient, help with homework versus no help with homework, allowing him to smoke pot versus trying to stop him from smoking pot—make no difference whatsoever? What if all those variables and many more like them JUST DON'T MATTER?

What if the real party is going on in another room down the hall? What if the factors that matter aren't strict versus lenient or helping with homework or not?

What if every kid is different? What if what works for one child is contraindicated for another? What if you have to know who your child is before you can help her?

I'll address this topic—at length—in subsequent essays.

19

Before going to the market, you know you want to pick up some groceries. But before going to college, many children and their families have only the vaguest idea of what they are "buying." College graduates earn twice as much over a lifetime as do their counterparts with only a high school education. No argument there. But that statistic doesn't answer the question why kids should go to college.

No Emotional ROI

"Why do you want to go to college?"

"To get a job."

This conversation, of which I've been a part well over a thousand times with my college counseling clients, is exactly backward. Indeed, the reason to go to college, the only reason to go to college, has always been because—wait for it—you don't need a job in the first place.

Before the Second World War, Harvard admitted two out of three applicants. This year, their admit ratio dropped from 6.9 percent down to 6.1 percent. About one in 16 win the lottery. In the competitive admissions cycle of today, applicants to Harvard write a composition of some 500 words for the common application as well as a shorter "significant activity" essay. Then there are supplemental essays.

Two generations ago, the entire Harvard application was only one question: "Does your father own land?"

Because if he did, Sonny was welcome to attend Harvard and to study philosophy, rhetoric, Greek, Latin, and other "practical" subjects.

"Honey wake up! I know it's two o'clock in the morning, but we have to call our philosopher!"

The purpose of college was the exact opposite of finding employment. The very act of going to college—liberal arts colleges anyway—defined students as people who didn't need jobs.

Jobs were for the working class. People who studied business, as opposed to liberal arts, needed to support themselves and their families. Why did they need to work to support themselves? Because their fathers didn't own land. Money was a taboo subject, never discussed.

"How much are the pork chops?"
"Lady, if you have to ask, you can't afford them."

Don't believe me? You think that people went to college to get skills to make a living? Then answer this question: How many Ivy League schools in 2013 offered an undergraduate business major?*

Do you want fries with that?

We have all met that kid who has an undergraduate degree in anthropology from Swarthmore—heck, for the purposes of this essay, let's give her a PhD in art history from Princeton—who can't get a job. "What are you going to do, teach?" is the equivalent of "Gee, for a fat girl, you don't sweat much." This question attacks the value of undergraduate education and undergraduates themselves and is offensive and demeaning at the same time. I'm a teacher, my wife is a teacher, my mom is a teacher, my mother-in-law is a teacher. We do okay.

Aristotle was asked by a student what the profit would be from learning. "He wants something for his learning," the teacher intoned. "Give him a penny." A scant 2,300 years later, the conversation hasn't changed.

"But we spent over $250,000 on Skidmore," parents of a recent Saratoga Springs grad lament. "And she's trying to find a job that pays $12 an hour." At that rate, it will take her just over ten years to earn back the cost of her education. If she lives at home. And never buys another app.

With the same quarter of a million dollars, here's what you could have done instead of "buying" a liberal arts education: you could have invested in a year of instruction in plumbing or another technical trade. Your daughter could be a skilled plumber and have a completely outfitted truck completely paid for.

I had a plumber here the other day. He was here for nine minutes. I wrote him a check for $230. Well worth it.

The purpose of a liberal arts undergraduate experience involves thinking about the questions that have engaged us these past few millennia. Neither Nero, Nietschze, nor Nash (Ogden or Graham) is part of the plumbing curriculum. We need to wake up and smell the pipes: plumbing is where the money is. College is where the value is.

The worth of an undergraduate liberal arts education can be valued but cannot be measured. There is no Emotional Return on Investment.

* Answer: Only one Ivy League School offers an undergraduate business major: The University of Pennsylvania. The closest Dartmouth, Brown, and the rest come to anything that could be said to be "practical" is a four-year degree in economics. No Ivy League school even offers a finance degree, never mind more traditional business subjects like management or marketing.

80

What is the purpose of sending our children to school? Are they learning information, or are they learning to be compliant? Are they learning to love reading, or are they learning to hate being in school?

Wake Up! It's Time for Your Sleeping Pill

Sam and Susie meet every day at noon at their brightly lit, air-conditioned gym. While walking on adjacent treadmills, they pass a bottle of designer water back and forth, chatting amicably about their families or events of the day. Sometimes they'll watch a favorite show on one of the abundant flat screen televisions while they lift weights. Sam and Susie chat about how many calories they've burned and how happy they are that they're staying fit. They agree that the greatest gift you can give to your kids is to stay healthy.

Kevin and Clarissa meet every day at noon on a dusty field littered with broken beer bottles. They carry CBS blocks back and forth in the heat of the Miami summer until their fingers bleed. Kevin and Clarissa do not understand why they are exercising or what the benefits might be. They carry the heavy blocks back and forth, avoiding the shards of glass, because they are told to do so. A paternalistic figure has said something they didn't quite understand about "bad cholesterol" and has threatened them with negative consequences should they put down their bricks. They are not allowed to speak.

Sam and Susie love "physical education." They look forward to their workout, the chance to stay healthy, chat, catch up on their TV shows, feel good about their progress.
Kevin and Clarissa, not so much.

Is there a difference between these two workouts? Is there a difference between making love on your honeymoon, thinking about starting a family, and, on the other hand, hitting a woman over the head and raping her in an alley?

***

At bedtime, five-year-old Katie brings her father *Fox in Socks*, their favorite book, and snuggles up under his arm. Dad reads, "When tweetle beetles fight, it's called a tweetle beetle battle." Katie giggles and pulls her blanket closer to her chest. Dad says, "If you pull the blanket, then we can see our toes.

Next door, a mother shouts at her kindergartener: "Eight o'clock! Bed! Now!"

Fast-forward ten years. Katie's geometry teacher is using the "if, then" construct. "If three points are non-collinear, then they determine a unique plane." Katie's computer science teacher is also talking about "if, then" statements in programming. So is Katie's philosophy teacher. Katie is as comfortable with "if, then" as she is with snuggling with her dad and a tweetle beetle battle.

The kid next door, the one who gets yelled at to get into bed? Again, not so much.

Which brings us—finally, you might say—to the subject of homework.

Why homework?

82

In a perfect world, homework is about learning. Kids who are excited to know what happens next in *The Giver, Island of the Blue Dolphins,* and *The Hobbit* will race home and read chapter after chapter. If they are not impeded by vacuous quizzes asking them to prove they've read only a certain chapter on a certain day, if they are not annoyed with stopping to write definitions of vocabulary words, if they are not tasked with dissecting and desiccating the books, they'll read, reflect, and learn.

In a perfect world, homework is about a shared journey: a teacher and a student, both of whom are interested in knowing how the world works, walking together in the direction of the joy of discovery.

In the real world, is the purpose of homework is to engender a love of learning? Probably not. Is the purpose of homework to help students learn? Nah. The purpose of homework is to demonstrate power and control, to give administrators a way to say, "Gotcha!" The purpose of homework is to allow teachers to say, "It's not my fault, Timmy didn't do well on the exam; he didn't do his homework."

Well, of course, Timmy didn't do his homework. If he were able to do his homework—the mind- numbing worksheets, the repetitive silliness—he wouldn't need to do it.

Homework is boring for kids who already know what they're doing. Homework is unhelpful for kids who don't.

In homes across the country, kids are learning, exploring, creating. They are coloring, trying to learn how to read, deriving their own meaning from their experience, wondering about how things work, trying to make sense of it all. They are learning from their parents, they are learning from their peers, they are learning by themselves. They are learning because they want to. Every child wants to learn. Until someone gives them a homework assignment. With homework—read only chapter two, do addition not subtraction, write these words ten times, memorize the names of the 67 counties in Florida— comes an agenda of power and control. Learn this how I say, when I say, and for no apparent reason. All over our communities, children have to stop learning—in order to do homework.

Wake up! It's time to take your sleeping pill!

If you can't forgive an old high school teacher for demonstrating some simple but elegant mathematics, you can skip right down to the part about how we are drugging our kids in ways that make the outcomes hard to predict.

Math and Parenting

Steven Hawking, who by all accounts knows more math than I do, relates in *A Brief History of Time* that his publisher told him that every mathematical equation he used in the book would cost him a number of readers. So he only used one equation. I'll do even better—no equations at all. And I promise I'll make a point about parenting too.

But first, some simple math: three people—Abercrombie, Bartholomew, and Clarissa—work together at an advertising agency. How many different ways can they make a presentation?

Well, they could all get up on stage together, all three of them. That's one way.

Or, they could split up into groups of two as follows:

Abercrombie and Bartholomew
Bartholomew and Clarissa
Abercrombie and Clarissa

So, there are three of these two-person groups.

Of course, they could just present individually. Abercrombie could take the stage alone. Or Bartholomew could. Or Clarissa. So that's three more ways.

And lastly, they could just do a "ghost presentation." No one could go up on stage. That would be a statement of some kind, I suppose. But nobody on the stage has to be counted as a unique way.

So, in total, there are eight different ways that three people can be grouped. One plus three plus three plus one equals eight.

But what if there were ten people instead of just three? What if we wanted to know how many different ways that ten people—Abercrombie, Bartholomew, Clarissa, Dysentery, Englebert, Felicity, Ganbaatar, Halcyon, Icarus, and Jagdesh—could make the presentation?

I don't want to list all the possible groupings of ten people. I don't even want to start thinking about whether or not I forgot to write down any of the groups of two. There are 45 of these groups of two. Never mind the groups of three—of which there are 120. There has to be a better way.

Which is where some simple arithmetic comes in.

To figure out how many groups of three there are, just multiply two by itself three times. Two times two times two is eight. That's the same eight we got by listing all the groups. (Not to be confused with two times three, which is six.) Two to the third or 2 ^ 3, is eight. There are eight ways to "combine" three people.

To figure out how many groups there are with ten folks, we multiply two times itself a bunch more times. Two times two times two times two times two times two times two times two times two times two. Another way to say this is "two raised to the tenth power," written 2 ^ 10. Two to the tenth power is just over a thousand. That's a lot of different groups.

Now—finally you might say—comes the parenting part. I met with the family of a high school student the other day. The young man was taking ten different medications. He was taking a psycho-stimulant for attention issues. He was taking a selective serotonin reuptake inhibitor (SSRI) for issues with depression and anxiety. He was taking an atypical anti-psychotic. He was taking a mood stabilizer. He was taking a benzodiazapine to help him sleep. He was taking four other medications, none of which I was familiar with. I seem to remember something about one medication being used to undo some side effect of two of the other medications. (Anyone remember all the verses to "I Know an Old Woman Who Swallowed a Fly"?)

Here's my question; see if you can answer it based on what you learned about Abercrombie, Bartholomew, Clarissa, Dysentery, Englebert, Felicity, Ganbaatar, Halcyon, Icarus, and Jagdesh: if a young man is taking ten different medications, how many different interactions are there between all those meds? If you answered "1024"—the same "two to the tenth power" as before—you get full credit. If you answered, "somebody needs to let this poor kid go out and play," you get an A+.

You did not go to live with your children. To the contrary, they came to live with you. Frequently, therefore, you are going to have to stand up and make the tough calls. It may be easier to make the hard decisions if the less desirable alternative is known.

Wanna Bet?

Which of the following responses seems more likely?

1) "Okay, mom. I'll turn off 'Shoot, Shoot, Shoot, Blood, Blood, Blood, Kill, Kill, Kill.' Gosh, have I been playing for 20 minutes already? I want to practice my bassoon then I want to get ahead on my schoolwork for next week. I think my teacher may be going on to Chapter Ten, and I don't want to be unprepared for her lecture on the Spanish Inquisition. You know how I like to read the chapter a couple of times before we start to learn about it in class. Thanks for the gentle reminder. Love you. I'll make dinner later so you can get some much deserved rest."

2) "What do you mean I have to turn off 'Shoot, Shoot, Shoot, Blood, Blood, Blood, Kill, Kill, Kill' and finish my homework? I have not been playing for nine consecutive hours! Nine hours? Are you kidding? I totally took a break to look at some Internet pornography and smoke some pot. You don't think those activities take time and attention, you stupid wretch? Nine hours? What is wrong with you? If you won't let me play 'Shoot, Shoot, Shoot, Blood, Blood, Blood, Kill, Kill, Kill,' I'll drink poison. It's all your fault anyway; I hate you."

How about these two?

1) "No, thank you, one beer is plenty. I want to get down to the homeless shelter to get in some more volunteer hours before meeting with my study group and besides, I'm underage."

2) "One more beer won't kill me. I drank 13 beers last Saturday before crashing my car into a tree and ending up in the emergency room with alcohol poisoning and a police record."

Think these examples are polemics? Think this is the Law of the Excluded Middle in action and that there aren't kids at these extremes? Think I don't see examples of both kids in my office every week?

Where does Kayla get the idea that she can skip school and meet friends at her parents' home during the day to drink beer and smoke pot? Is Kayla like Athena, born out of the brain of Zeus? Did she get this idea *ab ovo*?

Or is it more likely that there was a precedent, that somewhere along the line a little problem grew slowly and steadily into a bigger one? How many snowflakes does it take to cause an avalanche? Most IV drug abusers started their illegal drug use with marijuana, but the majority of marijuana smokers never go on to IV drugs. Both statements are true. How are you going to invest your limited influence over your children when they're still old enough to listen?

Here is some simple, straight-forward, directed advice regarding marijuana and beer for your kids: zero tolerance. No drugs or alcohol before age 25. (And when the kids get to be 25, we can talk again.)

Sure lots of kids smoke pot and grow up to be successful doctors, lawyers, butchers, bakers, and candlestick makers. But is that the smart way to bet?

Think of talking to your kids about drugs and alcohol as a negotiation. Start with zero. Zero is a good number. "We have a zero tolerance policy in our home regarding drugs and alcohol. Any questions?"

"But all the other kids are drinking."

"Yes, I've heard that, and I believe that's true." You may wish to pause here for dramatic effect. "But in our family, that's not how we do things."

There are 2.3 million people incarcerated in this country for drug-related offenses. Don't you think we should do everything we can to avoid having one of our children be number 2.3 million and one?

23

"Would you like to swing on a star, carry moonbeams home in a jar?" A generation ago, the absurdity of being someone who you're not was parodied in popular song. Today, parents routinely try to force their children into being who they are not.

Albert, Put Down the Violin!

Deborah, a gifted attorney, effortlessly writes air-tight appellate briefs. But ask her to speak in front of people in or out of the courtroom and she's so nervous that she can't sleep for days beforehand and wants to take Valium.

Anthony, a surgeon, was picked last for team sports throughout school. He still doesn't enjoy participating in athletics of any kind.

Winston's parents said, "There's no future in being an orator. We want you to excel at rugby."

Albert, a 25-year-old undistinguished employee of the Swiss Patent Office and an undistinguished violinist, is told by his parents to give up writing equations on the backs of envelopes and to stick to his music. (This never happened. But in the wrong family, it could have.)

Think about your skill set—what you're good at and what you love to do. Now, think about changing. If you hate talking to new people, imagine trying to make a living selling door to door. If you love all things numerical, imagine being forced to choose a career without math. Good counseling is about making a match between an adolescent's passions and abilities.

Our culture is full of examples of "overcoming adversity," of "triumphing over all odds," of three pointers at the buzzer, of kids staying up all night before the final and passing the course. Our culture is full of "Ordinary People," "Rudy," "Breaking Away," and "Stand and Deliver."

The reality is that in the examples above, it is the highly-trained, highly-motivated, highly-experienced athletes who make the miracle come-from-behind game winners. Kids in the classroom better be doing what they love, and loving what they do, because the reality is far less "theatrical." Kid who skip class all semester and then stay up all night and learn all the material are like shepherds. I hear about them a lot more than I run into them. Stated simply, kids who ignore their responsibilities all semester and then do well as the end are the exception. More frequently, these kids don't make it through.

I am a firm believer in the power of transformative positive change. I have been privileged to observe kids in recovery, adults who turn their lives around, 35-year-old women who go back to law school, addicts who get clean and become successful.

Here's what I don't see: Norbert, a talented musician, is struggling in science class. "If he just put in the same effort studying advanced chemistry as he does composing and performing music," his mom laments. "There's no reason why he couldn't be the top of the class."

Yes, there is a reason. Norbert hates advanced chemistry. He has no aptitude for advanced chemistry. He has no motivation to study advanced chemistry. Studying advanced chemistry is low on his list of priorities, somewhere between being lost in the woods and having an un-anesthetized colonoscopy. Could Norbert do well in advanced chemistry? I don't know. How many electric cattle prods does Norbert's mother own?

The army slogan is "Be all that you can be." But that's it. They don't go on to say, "Be More than You Can Be."

Think again about your skill set, what you're good at, what you love to do. Now think about being forced to change, to do something you hate.

Aren't you glad you are who you are?

24

There are always a hundred reasons to do the wrong thing, but only one reason to do the right thing. It is easy to come up with reasons not to donate blood. It is easy to come up with reasons why your son isn't doing well in school. Just the same, if you want your kids to grow up healthy, you have to help them choose the right path—no excuses, no prevarications.

The Only Game in Town

I asked a buddy of mine recently if he would join me in making a donation at the blood bank. He responded emphatically in the negative. "Why would you make a contribution to a corporation?" he began. "You're supporting a CEO who wastes money left and right. The head of the blood bank makes more money than you and I put together, and he's an idiot."

I know better than to interrupt Clyde when he's making a point, so I let him go on: "The guy has a boat, for goodness sake. Do you have a boat?" With a nod, I admitted that I was fresh out of boats. "He sells your donation for three hundred dollars."

"Whole blood is three hundred dollars," I interjected. "I give platelets. Platelets sell for closer to seven hundred dollars."

"See, that's what I'm talking about," Clyde continued. "You're sitting there with a needle in your arm for two hours so that guy can laze around on his boat? He's laughing at you."

"But..."

"I'm not finished," Clyde said. "Did you know that four years ago, the Red Cross was fined over four million dollars? They violated blood safety laws. Four million dollars. It was an incredible mess up. And you want to support this organization? You want to help make money for this guy so he can go out on his boat? Why don't you just send him $700 directly? There would be less stress and bother involved, and you wouldn't have to have a needle in your arm for two hours. Instead of lying there at the blood bank watching bad movies and eating stale cookies, why don't you just give him cash? That way he can pay his four million dollar fine and get some caviar for the next time he goes out on his boat."

Before I could respond, we were joined by Sarah, another friend from the neighborhood. "You think that blood bank guy is an idiot?" She began. "You want a real idiot? Let me tell you about the King of the Idiots. My son's sixth grade teacher is a complete and utter idiot."

"What's the latest?" Clyde asked.

"The man doesn't even have an actual teaching certificate. He has no classroom management skills; the kids are acting out all the time. It's impossible to learn in that classroom. There are close to 40 other kids."

Sarah went on: "You know how my son, Johnny, sometimes turns in his assignments late because he's up half the night playing video games?"

Clyde and I both nodded. Sarah talked about her son more than news anchors talked about news.

"Well then, get this: his idiot teacher lowered his grade on the assignment yesterday. Just because he turned it in late. Can you believe it? I mean, what difference does it make if the assignment is a few days late? The purpose of homework is for the kids to learn the material, right? What does it matter if my son is 13-years-old or 13-years-and-one-day-old when he learns this stuff? And the assignment is so stupid anyway. I don't know why anyone would be expected to know this."

Sarah turned to Clyde. "I mean, do you know anything about the Constitution of the United States? I certainly don't. Who cares? It's from like five hundred years ago. What difference does it make what happened in 1066?"

Clyde started to interrupt, but Sarah continued. "So I told my son what an idiot his teacher is. Maybe I shouldn't have done that. But I thought he had a right to know. What do you think?"

***

Here's what I think: There's a six-year-old in Chicago with leukemia. And a nine-year-old in Des Moines with aplastic anemia. And a 13-year-old in Baltimore with cancer. They need platelets. Otherwise, their quality of life is going to be bad. And then they're going to die.

In a perfect world, I would donate platelets to these kids directly. (I'm going to ignore for a minute the issue of just where I would get a $250,000 aphaeresis machine to process the platelets and a hematologist to put the needle in my arm.) I would cut out the middleman CEO with his huge salary and his boat. But in the real world, I can't get the platelets to these kids without the infrastructure—including all the waste—at the blood bank.

In a perfect world, Johnny's teacher would have better classroom management skills and there would be 20 students in his class rather than 40. In a perfect world, Sarah would acknowledge that there is something to be said for standing up and accepting that kids need to do the best they can in the situations in which they are placed.

Sarah's best parenting strategy would be to help her son understand that his classroom situation may not be perfect, but that he has to learn anyway. He needs to know that 1066, 1492, and 1776 are not adjoining rooms at a poorly designed hotel. Johnny's teacher may well be an idiot. But years down the road, "My teacher was an idiot" is going to be an inadequate answer when Johnny's knowledge and ability are being assessed.

Doubtless, there is a better way. And good people like you and me are fighting every day to decrease waste at the blood bank, to decrease class size, to educate parents about how to help their kids do the best they can with what they've got. In the meantime, I'll keep going to the blood bank if you'll keep helping your kids make their way in an imperfect world.

25

Why are some kids able to do so much more than others? Why are some kids able to do that which is helpful to them while others are only able to do that which is harmful to themselves and everyone around them? One theory of child development focuses on modeling—kids learn more from what their parents do than from what their parents say.

The Gifts We Have

Does your daughter know how to change the oil in her car?

Does your son know how to speak another language?

We spend time focusing on the academic profiles of our kids. My daughter has an A in Algebra II; my son is in the top ten percent of his class.

But can your son do his laundry? Can your daughter find her way across town in a strange city? Can your kids make a budget and stick to it in college?

Can they balance a checkbook? Can your son show up on time for a job interview? Can your daughter walk into a room full of strangers at a reception and start a conversation?

What about the skills that we would prefer our children not acquire? Can your son find the part of town where he can buy oxycontin illegally? Can your daughter steal a horse?

As loving parents, how do we help our kids get those abilities that will best serve them in an uncertain future?

The following well-known prose poem suggests that modeling is the answer for parents:

If a child lives with criticism, he learns to condemn.
If a child lives with hostility, he learns to fight.
If a child lives with fear, he learns to be afraid.
If a child lives with ridicule, he learns to be shy.
If a child lives with impatience, he learns to be hysterical.
If a child lives with anger, he learns to resent.
If a child lives with tolerance, he learns to be patient.
If a child lives with reassurance, he learns to be confident.
If a child lives with love, he learns to find love in others.
If a child lives with calmness, he learns to be at peace.

Similarly, if you smoke cigarettes, it is more likely that your children will smoke cigarettes. If you take illegal drugs, it is more likely that your children will take illegal drugs. (If you've been thinking about getting rid of that marijuana that you have tucked away up in your closet because your 11-year-old child isn't going to be naive forever, NOW would be a good day to throw it out. Yesterday might have been an even better time. I've never worked with a family in which the adults smoked pot but the children were unaware.)

In short, our children will likely do what we do, not what we say.

If you know how to scuba dive, take your kids scuba diving. If you know how to fix a tire, teach your kids how to fix a tire. If you know how to speak Spanish, teach your kids how to speak Spanish. If you know how to throw a ball, go have a game of catch with your kids. If you know the quadratic formula, teach your kids the quadratic formula. If you know how to build a fire, teach your kids how to build a fire. If you know how to bake muffins, teach your kids how to bake muffins. If you know how to bathe a dog, teach your kids how to bathe a dog.

Kids do learn what they live. The more time you spend with your kids doing stuff, the less time you'll have to spend telling them to do stuff.

The more time you spend with your kids, the less time your kids will have learning those lessons you don't want them to know.

A young person I know got a job tutoring. It was a crazy good job for this middle class, high school senior. The tutoring job paid much more than the minimum wage, and instead of bagging groceries or working outside in the Miami sun, the kid sat in an air-conditioned house and taught. The young person had soon saved enough from his wages to buy a computer and was saving up to travel around Central America after graduation.

Contrast this kid with the student who was given a Lexus for her 16th birthday but complained because she had wanted a BMW. Which student do you think will be more content? Which adolescent do you think will be more appreciative of what she has?

I asked the tutor how he was able to get and keep such a good job. "It isn't anything," he said. "I just teach my student the way my dad taught me."

"Cui bono" is Latin for "Who benefits?" Good parents make their own needs secondary to what is in the best interests of their children.

Oh, You Shouldn't Have

No list of "The Greatest Movies of All Time" is complete without including Orson Wells' 1940 *Citizen Kane*. The following dialog seems to predict conversations in my office 71 years after the film was produced:

KANE

As far as you're concerned, Susan, I've never wanted anything—I don't want anything now—except what you want.

SUSAN

What you want me to want, you mean. What you've decided I ought to

have—what you'd want if you were me. But you've never given me anything that... Oh, I don't mean the things you've given me—that don't mean anything to you. What's the difference between giving me a bracelet or giving somebody else a hundred thousand dollars for a statue you're going to keep crated up and never look at? It's only money. It doesn't mean anything. You're not really giving anything that belongs to you, that you care about. ... You've never given me anything. You've tried to buy me into giving you something. You're—(a sudden notion)—it's like you were bribing me! That's what it's been from the first moment I met you. No matter how much it cost you—your time, your money—that's what you've done with everybody you've ever known. Tried to bribe them!
...

KANE

(quietly) Whatever I do - I do - because I love you.

SUSAN

Love! You don't love anybody! Me or anybody else! You want to be loved—that's all you want!

***

Contrast the above conversation with one heard in the offices of imaginary* high school counselors around the country:

PARENT

He really is incredibly bright.

COUNSELOR

Tell me. Because the indicators of his ability tell another story. His grades are all Ds; none of his courses prepare him for college-level work; his norm referenced test scores are all below the national averages; he doesn't contribute in class; he doesn't read outside of class. Indeed, his only interests seem to be watching movies, being disrespectful, and skipping school.

PARENT

No, you must be mistaken. He truly is incredibly intelligent.

COUNSELOR

Can you give me any indicators of his aptitudes, abilities, or interests? Not everyone is good at academics. Does he work with his hands? Does he have good emotional intelligence? Is he good with people? Is he gifted athletically? Is he good with spatial relations? Does he help out around the house?

PARENT

No. But he's very smart.

COUNSELOR

I see.

***

Why is it so important for this parent to have a bright child? Would the parent love the child less if he just weren't that smart? Whose interests are served if the child is bright?

All loving parents want what is best for their children. All loving parents want their children to be bright, happy, and successful. (That their children also be compassionate, thoughtful, and helpful is the subject of another essay.)

It could be argued that the parent in the example above is more interested in telling colleagues at the country club about junior's abilities than he is in actually addressing junior's deficits. To whom is it important that the child be smart, the child or the parent?

And what about the student who truly is smart? If she truly is able, then she'll figure it out on her own without any ponderous insight: she'll read and be able to understand. She'll have a homework assignment and be able to figure it out. She'll run into a real life problem and come up with a real life solution. She won't need her parents to tell her she's smart.

***

Last example: When your four-month-old daughter was asleep, did you wake her up to cover her with kisses? Or did you let her get some rest knowing that what she needed was to sleep? As parents, we want our children to know that they are loved. The best way to show our love is to give our kids what they need. Not what we want them to need. Not what we want to give them.

The ability to make this distinction—between our children's needs and our own—is what separates good parents from early 20th century narcissistic newspaper moguls.

* "Imaginary" because counselors—concerned about litigation for themselves and their schools—don't typically speak in such a direct way.

Before making fun of the over-the-top narrator here, ask yourself if you fight battles for your child—battles that your child could learn to take care of without your help. Also, consider whether what you're fighting for is truly in your child's best interest. Maybe playing outdoors will allow your children to become self-reliant—even if she does risk minor injuries. As always, I hope the gentle sarcasm of this piece instructs rather than offends.

Gangrene

There's this wooded area behind the park down the street from our house. A couple of years ago, my 14-year-old daughter wanted to play there with her friends. Is she crazy? Anything could happen. There could be a beer bottle in the woods there. You never know. The beer bottle could be broken; my daughter could step on it; she could cut her foot; her foot could get infected; she could forget to take her antibiotics; she could get gangrene. The gangrene could spread; she could end up in the hospital; she might need to have her foot amputated.

She could end up a uni-dexter.

So I called the city. It took over a year and a half to get anything done, and I had to hire an attorney to file a class action suit. What a bother. But eventually I prevailed. The park and the wooded area behind it are now closed down. No one is allowed to go there anymore. What a relief.

One of the other mothers saw me in the market and said, "Now the children have no convenient place to play outdoors." What a loony that woman is. At least, as a result of my hard work, my children will have two feet.

This is the same mother who gave me attitude after I sued the pre-school ten years ago, got all those inept teachers fired, and had the place shut down. "They were loving, compassionate professionals doing the best job they could with limited resources," she whined.

What an idiot.

My daughter had been going to that lousy school for two full years and she still didn't know her multiplication tables. The four-year-olds were still learning their shapes and colors! Can you imagine? She didn't know the capitals of all 50 states. And they had the unmitigated temerity to put my gifted child in a heterogeneous classroom with three-year-olds. No wonder she graduated from pre-school without knowing how a bill becomes a law. Of course I had to sue the school and have them shut down. What else could I do? Incompetence has to be ferreted out and punished. Otherwise, as a result of these inept teachers, my daughter might not be Number One.

But did I get any gratitude from the community? No. Some stupid mother said, "Now the neighborhood children will have a longer commute to attend school." So what? At least at this other school, my child will be the best. That is, she will be the best if there are competent teachers who do what I tell them. Otherwise I'll get to work closing down that school as well.

I have my attorney on speed dial.

Now that my daughter is 16, she's been spending time outdoors—walking from the car to the house. I am very concerned about the possibility of skin cancer. But are the feckless local politicians willing to do anything about this threat? Of course not. So once again, I'm going to have to take the matter into my own hands. As usual, it may take some time and effort to effect what is in the best interests of my child, but I'm willing to do what it takes.

I'm going to sue the sun.

***

In short and without irony: this mom is not acting in the best interests of her child. She might think she is; she might feel strongly about it, but she's not. This mom is not allowing her child to figure things out on her own.

At our best, as parents, our sacred responsibility is to prepare our children to cope, to solve problems, to resolve issues. We need to help them make lemonade, sell it, invest the profits, and compost the rinds.

If the function of a good liberal arts education is to teach undergraduates to pose, research, resolve, and articulate problems, our duty as parents is to allow our children to be ready—cognitively, socially, and emotionally—to do so.

Litigating on behalf of our children is unlikely to allow them to achieve for themselves.
And before you dismiss the mother above as a figment of my fevered imagination, check out the story about the woman who sued the pre-school in New York because her daughter wasn't learning fast enough. That's right: "pre-school." As Dave Barry says, "You can't make this stuff up."

As much as we love our kids, as much as we want what's best for them, we can't clean up all the broken beer bottles in the world; we shouldn't destroy the career of every imperfect teacher; we can't bleach the outdoors.

A better plan would be to help our kids acquire the skills they need to overcome adversity and to take control of their own destinies—on their own.

28

We are taught in romantic movies that we can have it all—good relationships, good schools, good outcomes for all. The reality is harder. It takes time, hard work, and commitment to make a marriage work or to bring up healthy kids.

Passion

Her marriage of 20 years is stifling; her husband, an unfeeling clod. He is as insensitive to her needs as he is oblivious to her desires. In the months since they have been physically intimate, she feels herself growing ever more distant from the man whom she refers to as "that feckless boob." The stressors on her marriage—economic, logistical, and psychological—burden her and cannot be shared or lessened.

His marriage is even worse. His wife—the mother of his three children!— barely speaks to him. She is derisive rather than respectful. Even though he is an unfailing economic support, even though he has tried everything, even though he has offered to go to counseling, she doesn't even make an effort any more. Their meals are eaten in silence. Their marital bed is desolate.

The wife in the first paragraph above and the husband in the second paragraph meet. Their relationship develops with speed matched only by intensity. They feel for one another what they haven't felt for their spouses for years. They both know in their heart that this time it will be different, that this time they have met their soul mate, that this time the passion will last.

Through a series of subterfuges, deceptions, prevarications, and outright lies to their respective mates, they arrange a clandestine meeting in Aruba. On a deserted beach. Just the two of them. At sunset.

They sip a bottle of Chardonnay then—as if at an unspoken signal—collapse in one another's arms. They make mad love on the beach as the waves crash over their reborn bodies. Then, as the credits roll...

... Except this is real life, not a movie. There is no tidy happily ever after.

The next morning their clothes are sopping and they are both shivering— from cold not from desire. There is sand everywhere. Everywhere.

And someone has to get the kids to school, to soccer practice, to the orthodontist.

"Marry a good cook," we were told in previous generations. "Love fades."

***

Quick fix educational interventions make as much sense as extra-marital affairs as ways to resolve existing long-term issues. "We need to change text books; we need to change teachers; we need to change schools." "The situation is unpleasant; the situation is untenable; the situation is unbearable."

Staying in a broken marriage is as ill-advised as staying in an impossible educational setting. But before jumping to change for the sake of change, it pays to consider whether the alternative is better. Your math teacher may indeed be terrible. He may write with one hand, erase with the other, and mumble into the board all the while. He may not be nurturing, supportive, or a good communicator. He may be an insensitive lout: "Mr. Hart. Here is a dime. Call your mother and tell her that you will never be a mathematician."

Fitzgerald said, "Living well is the best revenge." Wouldn't the best way to get back at your math teacher be to do well in the class? If your math teacher is as much of a monster as you say, wouldn't he just hate it if you got an A? Rather than complaining, rather than switching classes, why not just do whatever it takes to get the job done? Go for extra help, hire a tutor, get a "study buddy," sit in on the class when it's offered during another period, do every problem on the homework twice, do every problem in the book three times. Do whatever it takes. Learn the material. "Hate the sin, not the sinner." "Hate the teacher, not the course work."

The best long-term marriages are not necessarily the most passionate. A dear friend was asked why she took care of her sick husband for 19 years until his death. In addition, she worked full time and raised three children. "He would have done the same for me," she said.

Change for the sake of change is a poor strategy in a marriage and in a math class.

And besides, getting an A in your horrible math class doesn't get seaweed on anything!

"The truth is a hard deer to hunt," says the narrator of Stephen Vincent Benet's "By the Waters of Babylon." Yet, it remains critical that the narratives we tell of our children's lives remain accurate. We gave birth to children, not to characters.

How the Story Changes

FALSTAFF

I have peppered two of them; two I am sure I have paid, two rogues in buckram suits. I tell thee what, Hal, if I tell thee a lie, spit in my face, Four rogues in buckram let drive at me—

PRINCE HENRY

What, four? thou saidst but two even now.

FALSTAFF

Four, Hal; I told thee four. These four came all a-front, and mainly thrust at me. I made me no more ado but took all their seven points in my target, thus.

PRINCE HENRY

Seven? why, there were but four even now.

FALSTAFF

Seven, by these hilts, or I am a villain else. These nine in buckram that I told thee of...

—The First Part of King Henry the Fourth, Act II, scene iv

Indeed, Falstaff has invented not only the ever-growing number of attackers, but also the entire battle itself. There was no actual battle. How the story changes within the space of a few lines.

"He didn't actually commit a burglary," a distraught mother explains in my office. "My son and a few of his buddies were just hanging out by the pool. They thought the house was unoccupied." Of course the police—who confiscated a dozen remote control garage door openers as well as drug paraphernalia—interpreted the situation differently.

By the time this mother is through telling the story, her son will be cast as part of a crew of do-gooders involved in volunteer home repair.

Wordsworth may have defined poetry as "emotion recollected in tranquility," but I'm more interested in the narratives I hear about adolescents.

Sometimes the story is exaggerated the other way. A parent makes out the situation to be worse than it is: "Suzy needs to go to boarding school immediately. Her grades have plummeted; she's drinking; she's out 'til all hours with horrible friends; we're at the end of our rope; we can't live like this."

Except it turns out that Suzy's grades have dipped from a 3.8 to a 3.5; she had a sip of beer at a family event; she missed curfew one time by 15 minutes. Suzy needs boarding school as much as Atlanta needs more kudzu.

By the time a situation reaches the court system, it's hard for me to determine what the truth ever was. In criminal court, there are typically people who have done bad things who are trying to appear good. In family court, there are people who haven't done much of anything at all, who are acting badly.

Bad divorces frequently involve absurd allegations from both parties, exaggerated to a literary degree: Mrs. Smith is deliberately turning my children against me; I'm accusing her of "parent alienation syndrome." Mr. Smith is a horrible father. He is inappropriate and abusive with the children.

I've known Mr. and Mrs. Smith since high school 40 years ago, and I've known their children since the day they were born. None of that ever happened; none of these allegations are true anywhere except on paper. Are Mr. and Mrs. Smith the best parents I've ever seen? Nah. Should the City of Coral Gables invest in a statue in the park as a tribute to the Smith family's abilities as care givers? Again, no. But their accusations grow as rapidly and as reasonably as the number of Falstaff's attackers.

Here's the reason that the family therapist told Mr. Smith not to insult Mrs. Smith in front of the children: the children are half her. When Mr. Smith remarks on what an idiot his ex-wife is, he is communicating to the children that they are idiots as well. After all, half their genetic make-up comes from their mom.

Mr. Smith would do better to diminish Mrs. Smith's failings, suggesting that her nine men in buckram suits were, in reality, only shadows. The truth may set you free, but in this case the truth will first make your children miserable.*

* "The truth will set you free, but first it will make you miserable" is inscribed on the wall in large letters at the Hyde School in Connecticut.

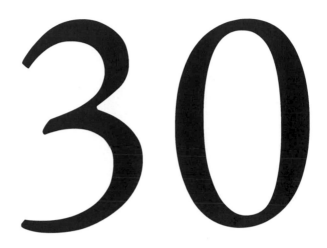

30

"One size fits all" parenting and "one size fits all" classroom education has been the rule in our country for generations. Some children thrive in a traditional classroom. But what about the ones who don't?

Save the Life of My Child, Part One

When Jackson's parents came to me asking "Is our child ADD?" my first instinct was to look at Jackson's curriculum rather than at his behavior. What Jackson is supposed to be learning and how he is supposed to be learning it may have more to do with how he is acting than might be apparent at first. Eight-year-old Jackson's behavior in the classroom and at home may be influenced by what and how he is being taught.

"Our kid is all over the place," Jackson's parents began. "He doesn't pay attention in school; he runs in the halls; he doesn't know what the homework is. And when we get home and finally get started on the homework, it's a battle of wills. We struggle for hours to get the worksheets done, and I don't think Jackson is learning anything." His thoughtful parents pause and reflect. "No, actually he is learning something," they go on. "He's learning to hate homework, to hate school, to hate us." Jackson's parents look at one another. "How do we get him to do his homework?"

Rather than address how to force Jackson to comply and do homework, my first question for Jackson's family is: "Is what Jackson is supposed to be doing for homework of interest to Jackson?" "Does his homework make sense to him on any level?"

***

I had an eighth grader in my office not so long ago who was required to memorize the names of the 67 counties in Florida.

The 67 counties in Florida. Can you imagine?

Why in the name of all that is good and decent in the world would anyone ever in a thousand years need to know the names of the 67 counties in Florida? A good buddy of mine is a judge. Do you think she knows the names of the 67 counties in Florida? I would venture to suggest that she does not. I myself certainly don't know the names of more than half a dozen counties in Florida and I'm considered pretty well educated.

Need the names of the 67 counties in Florida? Ever hear of the Internet? Type "counties in Florida" into Google and you'll have the list in under 12 nanoseconds.

So what is a concerned parent to do?

How do we force our children to comply with this assignment? We can make mnemonic devices. (ABB stands for Alachua, Bay, Bradford...) We can make a song. (I've always admired Tom Lehrer's rendition of "The Elements" to the tune of Gilbert and Sullivan's "Modern Major General.") We can use visualization imagery. ("Imagine a *Manatee* with an *Orange* in his mouth standing on a *Baker*...) We can promise. (If you learn the names of the 67 counties in Florida, I'll give you a pony.) We can threaten. (If you don't learn the names of the 67 counties in Florida, I'll take away your cell phone.) We can stand on our heads, but the short of it is that learning the names of the

67 counties in Florida is a completely stupid waste of time. I defy any teacher to justify this "lesson" as being good for children. Learning the names of the 67 counties in Florida.

Why would any child want to do that?

The agenda of this curriculum is about power and control. This lazy teacher communicates, "Learn what I say, how I say."

Now admittedly, it is easier to point out what's wrong with what teachers are doing in our children's classrooms than it is to develop and implement thoughtful curricula. And then there's the stupid FCAT in our state sucking time and creativity out of our teachers.

But how is this Jackson's problem?

Because now his situation starts to roll out of control. "He's learning disabled;" "He has attentional issues;" "He's oppositional;" "He refuses to learn;" And my favorite: "He chooses not to be a good student."

Please.

You go learn the names of the 67 counties in Florida. Spend a few hours of your precious young life memorizing this pointless information and tell me how you like it. Especially if, at eight years of age, memorizing is not what you do best.

So the question remains: is Jackson's curriculum interesting to Jackson? Because if his curriculum is "sit down and shut up," he just might not be too into it.

And don't tell me that much of education is learning material that doesn't seem relevant or interesting and that there's a lot of "learn this because I said so" coming down the road later on in life. There are a lot of pollutants in the "real world." That doesn't mean I should add asbestos and radon to the mashed yams.

Now, as it happens, I've known Jackson's father for 40 years, pretty much since the day he was born. I had a lot of respect for Jackson's grandfather (rest his soul), and I remain extremely fond of Jackson's grandmother. So I've been hanging out with Jackson's family for three generations beginning about the time that the Beatles came to America.

Jackson's father, I remember, used to be a pretty active kid—riding his bike up and down the street, working in the garden with his dad, playing cards with his mom. Jackson's dad is sharp as a tack, but never much liked sitting at a desk for seven hours either. I wonder if Jackson's dad learned in spite of what went on in his classroom rather than because of it.

Maybe Jackson's classroom is harmful rather than helpful to Jackson. Maybe not every eight-year-old child learns best sitting at a desk. Maybe Jackson can be forced to sit down, but not forced to learn.

31

Following is some advice for Jackson and his parents regarding the situations described in the previous chapter. As counterintuitive as it might at first appear to throw away the worksheets, the alternative of forcing the children to do them can be worse in the long term.

Save the Life of My Child, Part Two

In our last installment, Jackson was tied to the railroad tracks and the train was a' comin'. His mustachioed teacher had told him to learn the names of the 67 counties in Florida or he was going to lose the farm and miss recess.

"Sit down, shut up, and do this worksheet how I say, when I say," intoned Snidely Whiplash, grimacing down menacingly over our eight-year-old hero.

"But this curriculum of sitting all day isn't developmentally appropriate," rejoined Jackson. "And besides, I want to go play."

How can we get Jackson off the track of the train and back on track to love learning? Let's begin by forgetting about worksheets. Then, for Jackson, we may have to stop doing homework for a little while as well.

I know this sounds extreme especially in these days of "accountability," but hear me out: instead of forcing Jackson to read some vacuous passage and answer meaningless questions from a worksheet, have him curl up in Daddy's lap and pick out a book that he likes. Read it out loud to him. Don't ask him any questions other than, "What do you think will happen next?" and "What book would you like to read now?" Then take him to the library and allow him to pick out some more books. For the first six months of this program, don't pay attention to whether or not the books are "on grade level." Just make the time to read every single day, seven days a week. You find time to cook for the child; find the time to read.

In short, focus on your child's education. Not what your child is learning in school.

Remember how much you enjoyed Tolkien's *The Hobbit*? Could there be a better, more enticing landscape for children? A whole world filled with entire races of folks their size: hobbits, elves, and dwarves! Wizards and conquest, journeys and magic. How could any child not be enthralled and enchanted, desperate to hide under the covers with a flashlight determined to find out what happens next to Bilbo and his intrepid party? How could such a page-turner possibly be ruined? Would it even be possible for any teacher to destroy a child's rapt enjoyment of this popular volume which has SOLD MORE COPIES THAN ANY BOOK EXCEPT THE BIBLE?

Easy.

Here are three tried and true methods for destroying a child's interest in this exquisite book:

1) "In Chapter One, 21 dwarves appear at Bilbo's home. What are their names and in what order to they appear?

2) Read this book and I'll give you a dollar.

3) Here's a syringe. Shoot this heroin in your arm then decide whether you'd

prefer to read *The Hobbit* or play "Blood, Blood, Blood, Shoot, Shoot, Shoot, Kill, Kill, Kill."

Answers:

1) Nobody who loves this book remembers or cares which dwarves appear and in what order at Bilbo's house. This is a "Did you read the book?" bludgeon from a teacher who believes children should be answering vapid questions rather than enjoying a brilliant book.

2) Nothing destroys intrinsic motivation more than an external reward.

3) I'd rather eat chocolate than enjoy a healthy meal. That's why I stay away from chocolate. Similarly, most kids would rather play "Blood, Blood, Blood, Shoot, Shoot, Shoot, Kill, Kill, Kill" than read even the most wonderful books. That's why Jackson's parents shouldn't allow him to play video games.

Indeed, Jackson's parents need to throw out everything in their house with an on/off switch and a screen. Their computers need to be in public spaces (living room not bedroom.) Word processing and Internet research are okay. Computer games and Internet pornography, absolutely not.

Jackson needs to have the psychic space so that he can become a lifelong learner. The fewer distractions the better.

Because the train is a' comin'. And Jackson needs to learn to read, to read to learn, and to love to read.

32

"Present mirth hath present laughter." Writing college admissions essays for your children—another word for this practice is "cheating"—has long-term negative consequences. You not only undermine your child's sense of himself but also set yourself up for more cheating down the road.

Reciprocal, Stoic, Sycophantic, Aliens, Zebras!

Jonathan's profile is overflowing with modest grades in English and poor verbal test scores. He has never read a book that was not assigned and has overlooked many books that were. His most articulate replies in the classroom are mono-syllabic grunts, yet Jonathan's college admissions essays are replete with "plethoras," "turpitudes," and "obdurates."

I'm thinking his highly educated, yet equally misguided, mother wrote them.

Don't misunderstand: college admissions essays are the toughest academic obstacles many 17-year-olds have faced. Applicants feel they are being judged; they only have experience writing compositions, not personal essays; they are not sure how—or whether—to communicate their innermost thoughts and feelings. It's a tall order.

Just the same, I try to imagine the dinner table conversation in Jonathan's home: "Your father and I are sending you to college where you will take first-year composition classes and write papers. But we've written your college admissions essays for you."

"Why, Mom?"

"Because where you are admitted to college is more important than what is in your head."

"Uh, okay. Pass the bottle of Chateau Mouton Rothschild, please."

"But you know it's just for show. The bottle is empty."

"Yeah, Mom. I know."

***

You've met Jonathan and his parents. We all have. They were ahead of us in line at the amusement park when Jonathan was 14. His parents were coaching him about what to say to the ticket seller. "Tell him you're 12, so your ticket will cost $35 instead of $50."

Jonathan's parents may be sowing seeds for a crop they would prefer not to harvest. Some years later—now a senior in high school—Jonathan comes home late:

"Jonathan, you were supposed to be home by eleven o'clock."

"Sorry, Mom."

"It's well after midnight. What do you have to say for yourself?"

"The traffic was terrible. I-95 was backed up for miles. A 747 made an emergency landing on the interstate. I'm sure it was on the news. Didn't you see it? There may have been aliens involved. There were zebras everywhere."

121

"Are you kidding? Aliens? Zebras? That never happened! You're lying! Where did you learn to disregard the truth like that?"

"In line at the amusement park."

"I beg your pardon? We have ethics in this family. How much is your good name worth?"

"Fifteen dollars, Mom. Same as yours."

***

Their poor model of ethical behavior has had predicable consequences. Which is not to suggest that a stringent moral code is the only way to bring up ethical kids. And Lawrence Kohlberg would agree that there is a difference between prevaricating about age and lying about authorship. I'm only arguing that kids learn what they live and that "from apple trees, you don't get pears."

"But everybody is cheating," my college counseling clients tell me.

I do not dispute this claim.

Monica, a 20-year-old anthropology major at a college whose name you would recognize, tells me: "My roommate goes to fraternity parties, has seven glasses of wine, and goes home with someone new every Saturday night. She is disappointed and surprised when the young men don't call, but that's not what I wanted to ask you about. My question is about me. In my culture, we don't get drunk and have sex on the first date. Am I at a competitive disadvantage in the market place for boyfriends?"

"No, Monica," I would argue. "You are at a competitive disadvantage only for boys who drink seven glasses of wine and have sex on the first date." If you want to catch a trout, don't go fishing in a herring barrel. In the meantime, perhaps you could introduce your roommate to Jonathan.

***

What is there to be said for parents who write college entrance essays for

122

their high school seniors? As I have argued in these pages for some time: love your children for who they are, not for what they do. I have suggested that if parents love the kids they get, they'll get the kids they'll love. There's a line between encouraging your children to be their best selves and disparaging them for not being someone else.

Writing college admissions essays for your kids communicates that the essays they have written are just not good enough—a damaging idea to communicate to a student writing a personal essay for the first time.

And for the record: my colleagues in admissions offices can smell an essay written by a parent from across the room. The "plethoras," "turpitudes," and "obdurates" give them away every time.

33

We make a mistake when we believe that we must be all things to our kids. To the contrary, we need to model ethical behavior for them—every loving parent knows right from wrong—but we shouldn't pretend that we know the answer to every question about every subject. As long as our children love learning, they'll find the right teachers.

Don't Teach your Spouse to Drive

My orthodontist is a genius. There's no other word for it. He's also a decent and compassionate man. He not only has a successful private practice, he teaches other orthodontists advanced techniques. Some years ago, before we met Steve, I took my daughter to another orthodontist who basically recommended that we move all the teeth from the right side of her mouth to the left side then rip the top of her head off and replace her brain with a lawn mower engine. (Okay, I don't remember exactly what he said, but his recommendation involved hanging a weighted ball from one of her teeth and something about the Mexican Hat Dance.) Without ever hinting that we had received harmful advice from a graduate of the "Laurel and Hardy Drive-through School of Othodonture and Chimney Sweeping," Steve gently suggested that perhaps there was a more efficient, less expensive, and less intrusive solution.

To this day, every time my daughter flashes her perfect smile, I think of how indebted I am to this wonderful professional.

I saw Steve this morning. We're old family friends now, and I'm always pleased to catch up with him and his kids. His youngest, Darla, started eighth grade this year. Steve told me how much he enjoys spending time with her, but that when they study together there is a little friction. Steve put a positive spin on it. "She really sticks with an idea once it's in her head," he began. "Even if she gets it a little bit wrong, she's not one to be easily swayed."

"That's great," I agreed.

"Of course, I don't agree with all the information she brings home."

"No?"

"No. Somehow she got the idea that the maxillary is one bone. Of course, it's two."

"Hmm," I said, feeling fairly confident that the maxillary bone is not a Disney character but lacking more incisive information. Just the same, I nodded in agreement.

"But she doesn't believe me."

***

So there you have it: no one in South Florida knows as much about facial bones as Steve. No one. But his 13-year-old daughter doesn't believe him.

What do I think of this interaction as an educator? I think it's okay. Darla can have the wrong idea for a few minutes.

Don't misunderstand. I'm not in favor of misinformation. I believe strongly that information is power and that the more students know about pretty much everything, the better. It's important to know that the Earth is four-and-a-half-billion-years-old (as of this coming Thursday); it's important to be well read; it's important to have fundamental skills in many areas and sophisticated knowledge in as many disciplines as possible. It's critical to be able to pose, research, solve, and articulate the solutions to problems in a variety of fields.

But it's not imperative that we, as parents, be the ones to teach our kids.

***

We all want what's best for our kids. We all want our kids to be smart, to be well-liked, to be comfortable in their own bodies. We want our kids to be successful, happy, and thoughtful. (We also typically want our kids to be like us: to share our beliefs, values, outlooks and religions, but that's another column.) But we don't have to be the ones to teach them everything.

Remember Atticus Finch, arguably the greatest dad ever? Remember when Jem is angry with his dad because Atticus won't play football for the Methodists? Jem thinks his dad lacks ability and guts—until there's a rabid dog coming down the road, and Atticus is the one to take the shot. From Harper Lee's 1963 novel *To Kill a Mockingbird*:

Atticus said, "He's within range, Heck. You better get him before he goes down the side street—Lord knows who's around the corner. Go inside, Cal."

Calpurnia opened the screen door, latched it behind her, then unlatched it and held onto the hook. She tried to block Jem and me with her body, but we looked out from beneath her arms.

"Take him, Mr. Finch." Mr. Tate handed the rifle to Atticus; Jem and I nearly fainted.

"Don't waste time, Heck," said Atticus. "Go on."

"Mr. Finch, this is a one-shot job."

Atticus shook his head vehemently: "Don't just stand there, Heck! He won't wait all day for you—"

126

"For God's sake, Mr. Finch, look where he is! Miss and he'll go straight into the Radley house! I can't shoot that well and you know it!"

"I haven't shot a gun in thirty years—"

Mr. Tate almost threw the rifle at Atticus. "I'd feel mighty comfortable if you did now," he said.

***

Of course, Atticus was such a great dad that he doesn't actually exist outside of a work of fiction. But even Atticus, best parent of the 20th century, knows the limits of what he can do for his children. He models ethical behavior for them and seems at peace with the limits of his abilities. He reads to Scout. But Harper Lee makes no mention of Atticus helping Scout with her homework.

At the end of the book, the drunken, vengeful Bob Euwell attacks Jem. Before Boo Radley kills Euwell, Jem falls on his arm and it breaks. Boo carries Jem home, where they wait for the doctor. Atticus doesn't try to set his son's limb.

There is no shame in not being all things to all people. It's okay if you can't teach your kids math. You are not the only person on the Planet Earth who knows the quadratic formula. Even Steve, as brilliant as he is, is not the only person in our community who knows how many bones compose the maxillary.

It's okay if Jem doesn't know how great a shot his father is. It's okay if Darla doesn't know how great an orthodontist her father is. It's okay if our children have teachers and mentors outside their own families.

34

Almost all loving parents know what to do with a neuro-typical child who does well in school and develops normally. It is less clear how to bring up healthy children from populations that have been traditionally marginalized and ignored.

Tarzan and Me

"Tenderly Kala nursed her little waif, wondering silently why it did not gain strength and agility as did the little apes of other mothers. It was nearly a year from the time the little fellow came into her possession before he would walk alone, and as for climbing—my but how stupid he was!

Kala sometimes talked with the older females about her young hopeful, but none of them could understand how a child could be so slow and backward in learning to care for itself. Why, it could not even find food alone, and more than twelve moons had passed since Kala had come upon it…

Tublat, Kala's husband, was sorely vexed, and but for the females' careful watching would have put the child out of the way.

'He will never be a great ape,' he argued. 'Always will you have to carry him and protect him. What good will he be to the tribe? None; only a burden.' 'Let us leave him quietly sleeping among the tall grasses, that you may bear other and stronger apes to guard us in our old age.'"

***

Replace Kala in the paragraphs above with "loving mothers everywhere." Replace "Tublat" with "just about every wrong-headed oaf who has had anything to say about how to educate children with learning differences."

Sound familiar?

As it happens, Kala's "developmentally-delayed" child has different abilities than those of his fellows. He is the one—as it turns out—who can build fires, use a knife, communicate with other species. He also can make sense of, in Edgar Rice Burrows' wonderful phrase, the "little bugs" on the pages of his father's diaries.

But in the troop of apes where the SAT measures only leaping and fighting, Tarzan is almost left in the tall grass to die.

Present mirth hath present laughter.

Throwing away kids who learn differently or develop at a different pace is an old idea. But minions of kids suffer to this day. What about other populations? Who else has been deemed uneducable? Dr. Johnson wrote: "A woman's preaching is like a dog's walking on his hinder legs. It is not done well; but you are surprised to find it done at all."

Number of women in Johnson's classes at Pembroke College in Oxford, early 18th century: zero.

Year in which women were allowed to vote in the United States of American: 1920. Year in which there are more women than men in medical school in this country: 2013.

Let's make it personal: I flunked math in high school. My algebra teacher told me that he would pass me for the course—my grade was an F, but he could use his discretion to make it a D—if I promised never to take math again.

Perhaps this is a better story if the reader knows that I went on to get an undergraduate degree in math, took endless courses in statistics in graduate school, and taught math for 30 years before devoting myself full time to admissions counseling and working with special needs students.

But enough about me.

How many of your students have been labeled "smart but lazy"? How many of your children have been dismissed with "Mickey chooses not to turn in homework"? How many of our young people have been thrown away because they couldn't sit still, learn their letters by a certain age, make eye contact, hold a pencil correctly, pay attention, color within the lines?

"Smart but lazy" should be the beginning of a conversation, not the end of one.

Is it just hyperbole to suggest that we are leaving good kids to die in the tall grass? Without a modicum of insight and support, kids who learn differently are at significant risk. Consider the following paragraph from Dr. Edward Clarke's *Sex and Education*, 1873: a woman going to college cannot "retain uninjured health, and a future secure from neuralgia, uterine disease, hysteria, and other derangements of the nervous system."

Are we denying education to kids with learning differences to save them from uterine disease? Are we throwing away students with attentional issues so that we may bear stronger apes to guard us in our old age?

The list of productive people with learning differences or attentional issues continues to grow. It's a list to which I am pleased to add my own name.

35

No child is born wanting to fail, but there sure are a lot of kids who are having trouble adjusting in the classroom and at home. It's a shame to see so many unhappy families. Frequently, a single simple change is all it takes to help get a family back on track. Here are two narratives; one is from a mother, one from a teacher at a boarding school.

Who's Who

My son, Leon, is oppositional and defiant. I have the evaluation from the psychologist who wrote up what I told her. I'm starting to think he's definitely bi-polar. At the very least, he's seriously attention deficit.

Every homework assignment brings on a world war. Every single day. He refuses to even do assignments let alone study in advance for tests. He says the teacher doesn't tell them when the tests are. Can you imagine? I believe the teacher. Leon lies all the time to get out of doing his work. Of course, his grades are terrible. I've told him again and again how important his marks are in the eighth grade. Next year counts for college!

His behavior at home? Unbearable, thanks for asking. He won't clear the table after dinner never mind pick up his room. Yesterday, he rode his skateboard into the house. Unbelievable. A skateboard. Admittedly, I was in a terrible mood to begin with—my boss is an idiot and is always screaming at me for no reason—but Leon hadn't even told me where he was going when he left the house. He knows he's supposed to be home for dinner by six. These are tough times, and he knows how much I worry. Not to mention that his friends are low life idiots majoring in "pre-thug." I need to know where he is. Atlanta isn't safe like when I was growing up here years ago. So, anyway, he rides the skateboard right into the living room. We just had the wood floors redone; he knows how much that cost. I asked him politely to get off the stupid skateboard, but he refused. Maybe he didn't hear me with those lousy earphones—he listens to the most offensive music—but I had to grab him. We got into a tussle, and he pushed me. His own mother. And after all my sacrifice. He pushed me. I'm at my wits' end. I don't know what I'm going to do with that boy.

My husband is just about fed up. He may be thinking about leaving me and I don't know that I blame him. If my marriage fails, it will be all Leon's fault. He just won't listen.

***

Noel is my favorite advisee here at the boarding school where I am also his English teacher. In my class, he "gets it," makes insightful comments about the reading, is always prepared for discussion. He struggles in math but has asked to be seated in the first row and seeks out his teacher for extra help several days a week. He earned a B- on his most recent test on factoring quadratics, and he is studying constantly. We couldn't ask for more. His performance in the classroom is getting better and better.

In residential life, Noel is emerging as a leader. He makes the newer students feel at home. He helps out on the weekends when the boys clean the dorm and takes on the least glamorous assignments for himself. He is respectful to teachers, staff, and residential life. He looks us in the eye and says "thank you" several times a day.

132

He has tried out for the cross country team and, although he's not all that fast, he may end up as the captain when the kids vote next week. His peers respect him tremendously; he runs his heart out, and they admire that. And he's always encouraging the other runners—even the ones who don't go to our school. In short, a great kid. I'm glad he's a student here.

The funniest thing is that we almost didn't accept him as a student. We got this evaluation—"testing," I guess they call it—that said he was oppositional, defiant, maybe even bi-polar. There were pages and pages about how the kid didn't get along with his mom at all, about how they had been physically violent with one another. There was some ugly incident with a skateboard.

I have to tell you, I don't know who was being written up in those notes, because who I read about and the kid that I taught just can't be the same child. I really think there may have been a mistake because they even spelled his name wrong.

The psychologist got his name backwards: "Leon" and "Noel." Kinda funny if you think about it.

***

Why was Leon failing at both school and life in his home in suburban Atlanta? Why is he so thoroughly successful in his boarding school in the Northeast? Yes, this is the same child described by two observers—his mom and his teacher.

Any of the following reasons may have something to do with it:

The curriculum in Georgia wasn't meaningful to him. He wasn't able to connect with his teachers at his local middle school. The teachers in boarding school are "better," more caring and insightful. Leon needed a "break" from the family dynamic at home—a "parent-ectomy" if you will. Maybe Leon was able to take responsibility for his grades and his behavior when he was a thousand miles from home. Maybe Leon just "out-grew" his bad behaviors. Maybe he finally listened to his mom when she told him—for the hundredth time—that his grades were important. (I don't put much credence in the "He finally listened" scenario, but I'm not willing to leave out any possibilities.)

Maybe the moon was in Aquarius.

133

Sometimes a change is called for. If what you're doing isn't working, if you've given your parenting strategy your best shot, if you've given your parenting strategy a fair chance, maybe it's time to try something else. Change can be hard, but change can be necessary.

You owe it to yourself; you owe it to your family; you owe it to your child.

36

Sometimes the simplest, most obvious answer is the best. Or as Dr. Woodard was said to have told his medical students: "When you hear hoof beats behind you, don't expect to see a zebra."

That Explains It

I have an unexplainable situation here. I was hoping you could help me try to make some sense out of this. My 28-year-old, recently married secretary wrote me the following note: "Dear Mr. Altshuler," it reads. "My head hurts, and I have been throwing up. I am going to the doctor. What do you think it could be?"

It's a stumper. Here's another one, a situation I can't explain. Help me figure this out, would you please? My house smells like a gymnasium. There are dirty socks everywhere. Sweaty tee shirts with inexplicable slogans have sprouted like kudzu in the quarters of my four adolescent children. ("Our sport is your sport's punishment;" "Pain is weakness leaving the body;" "Your pace or mine?") Groceries have started disappearing at an alarming rate: I bought a dozen bananas yesterday. Today, they're all gone. My grocery bill looks like the Marshall Plan. I can't keep pasta on the shelf; it evaporates by the pound. And the most inexplicable of all? All four children return late from school, exhausted and non-communicative. They sleep like stones. They used to run around and play in the back yard; now they don't do anything except stagger through their homework and collapse into bed. Worst of all, they disappear every Saturday before the sun is even up only to show up again hours later covered with mud, smelling like goats, grinning triumphantly, and whispering to one another about "splits" and "PRs." It makes no sense: What do banana splits and public relations have to do with one another? Like I said, it's a befuddlement.

Complicated explanations include the children having been kidnapped by aliens. The more realistic and, in this case, blatantly accurate account is that they're all running cross country for their middle school and high school teams.

Indeed, cross country explains each and every particular: the sweaty clothing, the constantly hungry and worn out kids, the early morning workouts. "Splits" are mile times in a five- kilometer race. "PRs" are personal records. And, of course, the tee shirts ("No time-outs, no half-times, no breaks. The only true sport.") refer to cross country as well.

How could sensible parents miss these obvious signs? They couldn't. No one could. Just as no one could fail to infer that my 28-year-old, recently married secretary is pregnant.

But here's a situation that parents miss all the time. And the explanation is just as obvious:

My 16-year-old son is grouchy all the time. In middle school, he was loving and polite. Now he's surly and disrespectful. We used to love his friends; they would come over all the time. Now, he meets them "at the park" or who knows where. We seldom meet his friends and when we do they don't look us in the eye or talk much at all. Our son won't do homework, says he "doesn't have any" or that he has "already done it." Of course, his grades in school have plummeted. Worst of all, things keep disappearing from our house: there are a few pieces of jewelry that I can't seem to locate; I always seem to have fewer twenty-dollar bills in my purse. Our son comes home at all hours and sleeps the days away. He never helps out any more with work around the house or in the yard. What could possibly be wrong?

What's wrong is that this young man has an issue with substance abuse; there's no doubt about it. It's as clear as the Western sky. No other explanation takes care of the facts as cleanly. Whether or not the substance abuse has mutated into addiction or chemical dependency is unclear and unimportant for now, just as whether or not the cross country runners competed on fields or wooded paths at their last meet. Once substance abuse has been accepted as the working hypothesis, each and every particular makes sense: the missing jewelry and money, the lower grades, the non-communicative friends, the secrecy and the lying, everything.

This kid has been smoking pot every day—several times a day for a year. It's the only possible explanation. No other theory fits all the facts. Indeed, no other theory makes any sense at all.

Here's another explanation, one that is some time in the future for the family of the pot smoking young man described above: Once he has been clean and sober for a year, the grades, the choice of friends, the frictional family relationships will all start to heal.

I'd like to write more about the wonderful potential for this young man's recovery, but I'm off to the grocery store to buy more bananas and pasta. I'm all in favor of cross country running, mind you. But if I see a sign in one of the kids' rooms that reads: "26.2. Because 26.3 would be crazy," I'm selling the house and leaving no forwarding address.

37

It's easy to point a finger at bad parents. Nosey neighbors work backwards—
the kids are a mess; therefore the parents must have done something wrong.
If only it were that simple.

Twenty-five Cents Worth of Bad Parenting

Six–year-old Child: Mommy, may I go out and play?

Mommy: Shut up! We only had you to save the marriage.

***

The excerpt above is as far as I've gotten in my new book, *Parent
Ineffectiveness Training: How to Ensure that your Child Grows up to be, at
the Very Least, Miserably Unhappy & Quite Possibly a Burden to Society.*

I'm concerned about finding a publisher because:

1) The acronym, P.I.T., is clever but may not, in and of itself, sell all that many books. And the title, *Parent Ineffectiveness Training: How to Ensure that your Child Grows up to be, at the Very Least, Miserably Unhappy & Quite Possibly a Burden to Society* may be a tad long.

2) That's all I've written

3) Bad parenting just isn't that funny. Who would want to read a book about bad parenting? Frankly, I don't even want to write any more than those two lines.

But I do have some—hopefully—more insightful questions: from what kind of parents do the healthy children come? The simple answer: loving, married, sober, middle-class families where both parents take off work to coach soccer seems simplistic, inadequate, and easily refuted:

You and I both know lovely children whose parents are not all that supportive. And we know kids who are a mess whose parents are as supportive as can be.

You and I both know lovely children who are the products of divorced, blended, and other kinds of families. And we know kids who are a mess whose parents are happily married.

You and I both know lovely children whose parents have issues with drugs and alcohol. And we know kids who are a mess whose parents are clean and sober.

You and I both know lovely children whose parents have no money at all. And we know kids who are a mess whose families have enough money for whatever they want.

You and I both know lovely children whose parents don't coach soccer or even attend the games. And we know kids who are a mess whose parents are active and involved in the children's sports.

The questions, "What makes a good parent?" and "What guarantees are there that my kids will grow up content and fulfilled?" are beyond the scope of what is currently known. I suspect that the interplay between these few factors mentioned and dozens more might begin to give us some insight.

But I just want to address bad parenting. B-A-D. An analogy, if I may. The following is an actual conversation between a math teacher and a student, aged 17.

Me: What is the decimal equivalent of one fourth?

Student: I don't know.

Me: One fourth is the same as a quarter.

Student: Uh huh.

Me: How many pennies are there in a quarter of a dollar?

Student: I don't know.

Me: A quarter of a dollar is twenty-five cents. So one fourth written as a decimal would be...?

Student: I don't know. Point one four?

***

What is the parenting equivalent of not knowing that 1/4 = .25?

Here's one from a highly-educated, happily-married, professional woman in her late 40s: "I don't know why our 22-year-old daughter is pregnant again with the child of her mid-level drug dealing boyfriend. Her substance abuse issues—lots of Xanax every day—are moving toward chemical dependency and there's no pre-natal care whatsoever. I don't know why she has a problem with drugs. Whenever we smoke pot with her, we tell her to only use it in moderation like we do."

It's easy to point a finger, throw a stone, at this misguided mom. She smoked pot with her daughter? What a terrible mistake! It's no surprise that the daughter is addicted to Xanax.

It's the families about whom we say, "I don't know what they did wrong, but their kids are a mess" that are harder to explain.

38

Some of my clients over the past several decades have been gracious enough to suggest that I have all the answers. As the following essay will suggest, when it comes to parenting, I am making my best guesses along with everyone else.

Don't Teach your Daughter to Drive Either

Teaching math is not just what I do. Teaching math is who I am.

Teaching math is a source of pride to me, a craft if you will. Some people can build a canoe or do a backflip. I can teach math.

I can teach math to low-income students at the community college; I can teach math to privileged kids at a private day school. I can teach math one-on-one or in large lecture halls. Wake me up at two in the morning and I can teach math.

I can't teach physics or Spanish or any other subject. I can't build a canoe or do a backflip, but I can teach math to anybody anytime anywhere.

I love to teach math. I love the "aha!" moments when my students get it. I love it when my students understand a concept for the first time. I love it when my students feel good about learning math and feel good about themselves as a result. And if I may be forgiven for being proud, I love being able to teach math with more patience and more understanding than almost anybody else.

So imagine my consternation when my own daughter came to me with the following math question:

$$x + 3 = -5$$

This is a tough concept to teach, but after so many years, I feel pretty good about my ability to explain it. To anybody. Like I said.

Here's what I was going to say: "Put a negative three on both sides of the equal sign. An equal sign is like a balance scale. Negative three is the same as negative three." Then I was going to talk about how to add two negative numbers together. "Negative three plus negative five is like when the temperature is three degrees below zero and then gets five degrees colder." I was going to draw a number line and give more examples.

Except that I only got as far as "Puh."

Not the whole word "put" as in "put the negative three on both sides of the equal sign." Just "Puh." I had only got as far as "puh" before my daughter interrupted and said, "That's not the way we learn it in school!" and left the room. In tears.

So I had a couple choices. My first thought was to chase after her screaming, "People pay me hundreds of dollars to teach math! I've been teaching math for decades! I can teach math to anybody! Come back here! You're out of the will!"

My other choice was to take the dog for a long walk.

I'm proud to say that I chose the dog walk.

I am less proud to say that I gave a lot of thought to the psychotic, raving, screaming choice before going to get the leash. I'm thinking that any dad who has ever tried to teach his kid some math can share my feeling.

***

If the choice is for me to teach my daughter math or to pay someone else to do it, I'd prefer to teach her myself. I wish we had the kind of relationship where dad and daughter could sit down together and learn math.

But we don't.

So instead, I pay someone else to teach my daughter math. (Taxes for the public schools, tuition for the private schools, tutors. One way or another, we pay.)

I also pay for someone else to teach my children physics and Spanish. If there were time in the day, I'd pay someone to teach my daughter how to build a canoe and do a backflip as well.

Note that teaching your daughter how to do math is different from teaching your daughter to put gas in the car or to take out the garbage. Chores around the house are non-negotiable. Everyone has to pitch in, do her share. Learning math is not optional; teaching your daughter math is.

There are many examples of "false choice" in education and in parenting.

I would rather have my kids read Virgil in the original Latin than in an English translation. The advantages of knowing Latin are legendary: an understanding of the structure of language, an impressive familiarity with the roots of English, a connection with an important culture, the list goes on.

But having students read Latin in the original versus reading English translations isn't my choice. My choice is to have my kids read Latin in translation or not at all.

144

Here again, my choice is clear. Of course, I'd much rather have the kids know something of the culture and literature than nothing.

In a perfect world, my daughter would love to learn math and I would be the one to teach her. I see no indications, however, that the world is heading in the direction of perfect any time soon. In the meantime, I happy to settle for second best.

39

How much of our problems with our kids are "self-inflicted"? How many of them are real? How much better would our lives and the lives or our children be if we could learn to take a step back, to "let go" a little bit?

Footing the Anxiety Bill

My foot itches.

I think I maybe got bit by a mosquito, but it could be foot cancer. You never know. I heard about a woman who had foot cancer. I've tried scratching my foot and then I tried soaking my foot in strawberry jam while scratching my left ear with my right hand, but nothing seems to work. Now my foot doesn't just itch, it hurts.

So I went to my doctor. He said that if I left my foot alone, it would stop itching and get better. He said that I probably had been bitten by a mosquito.

Idiot! Fool! Nincompoop! Which matchbox gave him his medical degree? Leave it alone? What a maroon! Doesn't he know anything about foot cancer! Stop scratching it? That's the stupidest thing I've ever heard. So I went to a specialist.

Who told me the same thing. "Stop scratching your foot and you'll be fine," she said. "Strawberry jam is unlikely to make your foot feel better and could very well make it worse." Collusion! Conspiracy! Clearly, those two charlatans are in cahoots. I'll bring them up on charges. I'll turn them in to the Medical Malpractice Foot Fraud Conspiracy Committee.

But in the meantime, I have to do something because, obviously, I'm on my own in that the entire medical community is aligned against me. I have to take my foot into my own hands, so to speak. So I went to the gardening store and bought a rake and started scratching my foot with the rake. But that only made my foot hurt worse. Fortunately, at the same gardening store, there's a machete I can buy. I'm going to make this foot stop hurting or know the reason why not! No series of incompetent doctors and their bad advice is going to come between me and my God given right to have a foot that doesn't itch. Ah, here we go. This machete looks to be just about the right size…

***

I'm having problems with my 14-year-old daughter. She doesn't want to do anything. She just mopes around the house reading books, making cookies, having her friends over to play Parcheesi. It's hard enough keeping this 6000-square-foot house organized—half my household staff are idiots—without worrying about my daughter all the time. The other day, I didn't know where they were. It turned out that they had ridden their bikes to the forest on the edge of town and gone for a hike and eaten some sandwiches. Can you imagine? Sandwiches and hiking of all things. So I put her in soccer. She doesn't like soccer; it's a struggle to get her up and out of the house. She says the other girls are ultra-competitive and mean. But she has to do something and all the other moms on my street are taking their daughters to soccer. Plus, I read somewhere that soccer is good for children. I've certainly never read anywhere that playing Parcheesi is good for children. And hiking? You could get bit by a mosquito. Which I'm pretty sure could result in foot cancer.

***

How many of our problems are "self-inflicted" and how many are caused by those around us? The woman in the first paragraph above is making her own life harder—and more painful—than it needs to be. The mother in the second paragraph is making her daughter's life miserable. Her daughter sounds fine to me. For the chronically irony impaired, let me state in a straight-forward way: the woman who got bitten by the mosquito should stop making things worse by trying to make them better. The woman in the second paragraph should leave her daughter alone. All those things her daughter is doing—reading, baking, chatting, bike riding, and hiking—are developmentally appropriate. If the child doesn't want to play soccer, she should not be forced to do so. There are many roads to Rome—some of which even pass through the woods on the edge of town.

In our culture, it is hard to differentiate what is healthy and appropriate for our kids from what is harmful. Here—again without irony—are my straight forward suggestions:

If your children are taking unprescribed Xanax, you have a problem that is unlikely to go away without intervention. If your children are oppositional, defiant, angry, and depressed, it's probably time to seek professional help.

If, on the other hand, your kids would prefer to read books rather than play organized sports, that's probably okay. You might even consider being grateful.

***

I got a ride with a Haitian cab driver in New York not long after the earthquake had devastated his already impoverished country. Feeling I should say some words of commiseration, I awkwardly muttered how sorry I was and that I hoped that he and his family had not been affected too much by the catastrophe. The cab driver thanked me graciously and said that he had indeed lost one of his three children in the disaster, but that he felt blessed because he knew of other families who had lost all their children.

I learned more from that cab driver than I did from the woman with the 6000–square-foot house. I hope you'll agree that your glass is just about full to the point of overflowing, your imperfect children and your bug bites notwithstanding.

148

Sometimes it's easy and obvious to know what to do to help bring up healthy, contented children in our homes. But what about the kids down the street? No story has engendered as much controversy as the following.

Smoking Ethics Question

I spend quite a bit of time in the neighborhood of one of my running buddies, not so many miles from my house. Before we go for our run, we meet with our dogs in a vacant lot near his home to chat, stretch, and watch the dogs romp. Last Saturday afternoon, Langley and I happened to get to the lot first. I saw Max, a kid I know from the neighborhood, and two 14-year-old girls whom I did not know sitting with their backs to me as I walked around the fence into the otherwise deserted lot.

From fifty feet away, I thought I saw Max smoking something. As I took a few steps closer, he turned around and saw me. I thought I saw him put a marijuana pipe into a backpack on his lap. I am not absolutely certain that I observed Max either smoking or putting a marijuana pipe into a backpack.

My question for my community of readers is: What is my duty, if any, to disclose to Max's parents what I think I observed?

If you argue that I should not say anything to Max's parents, would your answer change if I were more certain of what I had seen?

If you argue that I should communicate with Max's parents, would your answer change if I were less certain of what I observed?

Is my relationship with Max's parents relevant to your thinking about whether or not I should disclose? As it happens, I know them well enough from walking my dog through my friend's neighborhood. Although they don't have a dog themselves, they seem to like dogs well enough, and we've chatted over the years about the weather, sports, and politics. We could certainly not be described as close friends. I have never been inside their house. We have never shared a meal together.

If you feel that I should not communicate with Max's parents, would you change your mind if we could somehow see into the future and know that Max, as a kid with serious substance abuse issues some years from now, would get behind the wheel of a car and kill someone? If you feel that I should talk to Max's parents, would you change your mind if you could look into the future and know that Max was smoking marijuana for the last time?

Would your answer change if Max were 25–years-old rather than 14?
Would your answer change if Max weren't 14 years old, but 12?

Most importantly, if you feel that I should say something, how do you recommend that I go about it? "Hi, Mr. and Mrs. Murgatroid, I'm not certain, but I think your son was smoking pot the other day in the vacant lot near your house" just doesn't quite seem to cut it.

Although I have changed the details to preserve anonymity, the situation described above is all too real. All of us parents know who the pot smoking kids are at our children's high schools and colleges. It's not a secret. Go on their social media sites, for goodness sake; all the information is right there.

That glassy eyed kid in the picture? The one holding the bong? He has been smoking marijuana. Count on it. Go ahead and mortgage the farm.

If you believe, as I do, that marijuana use in 14-year-olds is a bad plan, what is your duty to the children of your friends and neighbors? When, if ever, should you communicate what you know? How should you say what needs to be said?

Sometimes parents have to stand up and be the parents. It's not easy and it's not fun and it's not a short-term commitment either. If you would allow your 14-year-old child to drink a great deal of alcohol, you may wish to skip this essay; you won't be pleased with the advice.

Typo!

Maybe I shouldn't, but I let my 14-year-old son drink alcohol every day. Usually I just let him have beer, but sometimes I let him drink vodka or bourbon. I let him make his own decision; it's his choice. He'll be an adult soon, and there is a lot of alcohol in the world. The sooner he is able to determine for himself how much alcohol he can drink and what kind of alcohol works best for him, the better.

Of course I'm aware of the research that says that alcohol destroys the adolescent brain and that neuronal development keeps going until age 25. Of course I know that the longer kids stay away from alcohol the more likely

152

they are to be successful by every objective measure. The research is unassailable, true. The earlier kids start drinking, the more likely they are to become alcoholics as adults.

But there are lots of kids in our neighborhood who are drinking alcohol at 14. I don't want my son to be different.

Here's my most cogent argument for why I allow my 14-year-old son to drink alcohol as much as he wants: he's really good at it.

He doesn't like to read; he's not doing well in school; he doesn't have any other interests besides alcohol. I tried to get him involved in sports and activities with other children. I tried to get him interested in community service or helping the kids who do work with Habitat for Humanity, but he didn't want to. He has trouble fitting in socially, always has. Drinking alcohol is what he does best. It gives him a sense of confidence and ability. Without alcohol, I think his self-esteem would be even lower. Who am I to take away the thing that he's best at, that makes him feel good about himself?

I tried to get him to cut down, but it just didn't work. I said that he could only drink alcohol for three hours a day, that six hours a day of drinking alcohol was too much. But we just got in a big fight and it wasn't worth the trouble. The fact of the matter is that as long as he drinks alcohol, we get along okay. Sure, he's grumpy and non-communicative even when he drinks every day; yes, he's surly and disrespectful. But at least he's not cursing at me and shoving me. When I tried to take away the alcohol, he said he would harm himself. If he hurt himself I just don't know how I could live with myself.

One of my friends asked me how my son got started with alcohol to begin with. I have to admit that I might be at fault. When he was four years old, we were at a restaurant and he was misbehaving, throwing a tantrum really. I didn't feel like I had any options. I gave him some crayons, but he didn't want to color. He wouldn't sit still. I didn't want to ruin the evening by taking him home. So I gave him some alcohol. Just a little bit to get him to calm down and behave himself. I guess the situation just grew from there. Whenever he would misbehave, I would just give him a little alcohol and he would calm right down. Of course, over time, it took more and more alcohol to get him to behave himself. I guess I made a mistake, but now there just doesn't seem to be a way to go back. I still don't see what I could have done differently. One thing just followed another and here we are.

I wonder what the situation is going to be like in four years when my son is 18. I don't know if he'll be able to get into a good college. His grades in ninth grade aren't good at all, and I don't know how well he can be expected to do in college what with his drinking alcohol all the time.

***

David here, no longer channeling the parent whom I was quoting above. It seems I have made a mistake in my transcription of the conversation. I made a consistent and glaring typographical error. The parent didn't actually say "alcohol" in the paragraphs above.

What the parent said was "video games."

I'll rewrite with the correction in place:

We started our son playing video games when he was four years old. We were at a restaurant and the interactive screen was the only thing that would calm him down, keep him from throwing a tantrum. We both work so there wasn't time for board games, reading books, going for hikes, or playing in the back yard and besides, the video game was what he preferred. Over time, we came to prefer the video game as well. It kept our son quiet and allowed us to get our work done. It's hard enough to cook dinner without having a four-year-old crawling all over everywhere, asking questions, trying to "help", getting in the way. With a screen in front of him, he was well behaved. I was able to get some rest after a full day as well. Then the battle to get him off the game became untenable. Getting him to cut down was no use. He was happier in his virtual world than he was in the real one.

***

Here, stated explicitly and without irony, is my opinion of video games:

Some can; some can't.

That is to say, there may be kids who can keep it under control, only play for a little while then put it away. If their grades are good, their social

154

interactions are viable, and they're getting enough exercise, then I don't have a problem with video games. I'd rather take my kids camping than have them play video games, but I acknowledge that the two are not mutually exclusive and that not everyone likes sleeping outdoors.

Just like alcohol, some people can have a glass of wine at dinner on the weekends and never have an issue with alcohol. If the kid is otherwise healthy and happy, I suppose a little bit of video gaming now and again might not hurt.

It doesn't impress me as the safe way to bet though.

I know all about your friend who smoked cigarettes from the time he was 13 until he died of causes unrelated to smoking at age 92. Your friend's happy, healthy life is not a good argument in favor of taking up smoking. In statistics, these arguments that disregard the denominator—in this case the number of people who die painful deaths due to emphysema—are called "whistling past the cemetery." That is, the people who started smoking cigarettes at 13 but didn't live to 92 aren't around to tell their stories.

You wouldn't give your 14-year-old son alcohol. Not even a little. Don't give him a video game either. You know the old expression, "Pay me now or pay me later"?

Now is cheaper.

Suffer through the tantrums. Suffer through paying attention to your kid and the difficulties of parenting. Have a conversation. Heck, have an argument. Say what you think and let your kid say what he thinks. Sunshine is a powerful antiseptic.

And a video game is a potentially very bad drug.

All loving parents want their children to absorb their values and beliefs about politics, religion, and morality. Sure, we want our kids to be better than we are. But we also want them to share what is most important to us. How to get our kids to internalize that about which we care most deeply is the tricky bit.

The Beatings Will Continue Until Morale Improves

I felt strongly about a recent election. In my judgment, Candidate A was the better man. Candidate B had his good points, certainly, but Candidate A had my unqualified support. I was so thoroughly convinced that Candidate A would be a more effective leader that I went downtown to his campaign headquarters to make a small monetary contribution and to pick up a sign to put in my yard.

After thanking the young campaign workers who graciously accepted my check and gave me a campaign poster, I started toward my car, concerned

156

about the time on the meter and about getting back to the office. Before I could take a step, however, the campaign manager approached me and started telling me about the policies and opinions of the candidate whom we both supported. As it happened, I agreed with all the policies and opinions being espoused, so I didn't mind listening and nodding my head. But as the lecture turned into a harangue, my desire to make sure I didn't get a parking ticket increased. It became clear that I wasn't part of a discussion about ideas. Indeed, I wasn't sure that my presence was even a necessary part of the endless stream of verbiage. I glanced repeatedly at my watch as the minutes and the arguments crawled by. On and on the vitriolic stream of information roared: "Candidate A has good policies! Candidate B is a bad man!" Finally, I interrupted the diatribe and excused myself.

"Candidate B will ruin our country," the campaign manager yelled after my rapidly retreating back. "Don't forget to vote for Candidate A!"

For the first time in my life, I considered changing political parties.

I have never missed an election since I started voting in 1968. I have never voted for the political party of Candidate B, but I was sufficiently annoyed, after the incessantly yelling, to consider it.

What was so viscerally disagreeable about being lectured to—even about positions with which I was in complete agreement—that I was annoyed enough to consider voting for the other guy?

And what does an insensitive campaign manager have to do with my usual topics of education and parenting?

I thought you'd never ask.

***

Teachers and parents are in the convincing business. Think about it. From potty training to the Pythagorean Theorem, our sacred duty is to transmit our values to our children. That's our most important job as parents. If we don't communicate our values, we can be assured that someone else will assert theirs. The question, of course, is how to go about convincing our kids that what we have to say is valid and worthy of emulation.

157

Our motivation is critical. Even a stray dog knows whether he has been tripped over or kicked. A hidden agenda of "learn this because I said so" is less cogent than "here's something I think is worth knowing and you might too."

That's why we remember our enthusiastic teachers more fondly than our fascistic ones.

And "do as I say, not as I do" doesn't get much traction. Dads who smoke cigarettes are more likely to have kids who smoke. Dads who read are more likely to have kids who read. Modeling behavior is more likely to be effective than talking about it.

Sometimes the agenda of those in power is only too clear. Imagine a classroom of engaged students discussing a book that they have all read and loved. The teacher gently guides the interaction, involving each child in a deep examination of character, tone, style, and irony. Students are seamlessly learning literary terms and a love of literature…when an announcement comes over the public address system: "Beat Killian High! Come on out on Friday night to support your school. Buy 'Kill the Cougars' buttons!"

Not to put too fine a point on it, but the message here is clear: nothing that goes on in the classroom is as important as an Orwellian emphasis on beating some other school at an endeavor involving an ovoid object.

Once again, students (who, in many regards, are just like people!) don't respond well to being TOLD. If an obnoxious campaign manager can almost convince me to vote for the other guy, can't an overbearing administration work contrary to the interests of students? Similarly, can't a school system that emphasizes testing over learning turn off a generation of students? Most kids can grow to love reading; few will grow to love being tested.

43

In these uncertain times, we all want what's best for our kids. How to help them be successful in and out of the classroom is the more difficult question. Allowing them to find themselves and to excel at being who they are is the sacred duty of loving parents. Forcing them to be who they're not sends a debilitating message, one leading to psychic stress.

It's the Anxiety, Stupid

Not so many generations ago, musicians in general, and fiddlers in particular, were considered to be time wasters of the worst sort. Idle hands were the devil's playthings; those hands on musical instruments were the least productive. Music was considered the "gateway drug" to alcohol, dissolution, and shame.

Today, frantic parents go to war with their nine-year-olds over piano practice. It would be difficult to overstate the level of animosity and arguing regarding practice time. Bribes and punishments, threats and rewards, coercion and incentives are handed out like M&M candies and electric shocks. To what purpose? Do YOU know any employed musicians?

Neither do I.

Okay, I take that back. There's that nice trumpet player around the corner— great musician, great dad, all around good guy. What I meant to say was, do you know any happily employed musicians who were forced to play music by overbearing parents? Do you know any successful musicians who were coerced into a career in music even though they had neither aptitude nor affection for the discipline? Of course not.

If you are, gentle reader, a musician, try to imagine your life without your instrument, your friends with whom you love to play music, your study of that which you love.

And if you are tone deaf with clunky fingers and leaden hands, envision being forced to play.

Neither of these scenarios is imaginable, let alone feasible. Musicians have to play music. Non-musicians can't and don't.

Parents can model a love of music; parents can encourage; parents can push their children, gently, toward music. Parents can make good musicians better. But when the household is held hostage to arguments about the number of times a scale has been practiced, it's time to bring the baby back inside. Bathwater optional.

***

Consider a parent who takes turns yelling these contradictory phrases: go out and play! Come in and study!

Stay awake and do your homework! Go to bed, you're not getting enough rest!

Study your trigonometry! Stop studying trigonometry!

Stop learning this! Start learning that!

160

What if the proverbial "none of the above" is the right answer to all these mindless exhortations? What if allowing children to find their own way — even if they stumble now and again along the path—is the only way to help them grow up happy, content, and on the way to what Maslow called "self-actualized"?

Love the kids you get and you'll get the kids you'll love.

Rather than forcing non-musical kids to play music, rather than forcing musical kids to give up music, maybe parents should find their children where they are. Maybe the medium is indeed the message. Maybe kids don't hear "play trombone" or "don't play trombone." Maybe all kids hear is "don't be who you are." Maybe the only agenda that comes through is "I'm anxious and uncomfortable in my own skin, and you should be too."

What are your children able to do? How are you preparing them for the challenges ahead?

Resiliency is a B'ar

My family and I were at a restaurant recently, where we observed a nine-year-old at dinner with his family. The young man was intensely connected to his screen, suckling greedily on his video game. Both hands were cemented to the keyboard; his headphones were successfully obliterating any stimulus not generated by his handheld.

I was too many tables away to discern whether the young man was playing "Shoot, Shoot, Shoot, Blood, Blood, Blood, Kill, Kill, Kill" or some other equally enlightening video game; however, I was close enough to easily observe that a woman, presumably this child's mother, was feeding him French fries.

If resiliency is defined not by how many times you fall, but by how many times you get back up, what predictions can be made about how able an adult this young man is likely to become?

My guess is that this young man will not grow up to be especially resilient. Were I a snarky sort of person, I would remark that this young man might someday, with a little luck, develop the ability to eat French fries on his own.

Of course, one can never be certain.

***

Mom: I'm concerned about my son.

Another Mom: Oh? What's wrong?

Mom: He watches "Barney" three times a day, five days a week. He watches "Barney" before breakfast and again in the afternoon. He's seen every episode again and again. He'd rather watch "Barney" than do almost anything else.

Another Mom: Yeah, my kids love "Barney" too. It's not a bad show. Barney teaches kids to brush their teeth and to clean up after themselves.

Mom: I know. But my son is 29.

***

The time to allow your physically-able children to feed themselves is before nine years of age.

The time to stop your children from playing video games is yesterday.

The mother feeding her son French fries would doubtless justify her action: "He needs to eat," she might begin.

No argument there.

But at the same time, you have to agree that there is something desperately wrong with the picture of an able-bodied nine-year-old completely disengaged from meaningful human contact, isolated from his family, ignoring any interaction with wait staff, being fed French fries.

The child may as well have been on Neptune.

Back here on *terra firma*, sensible parents want our children to be able to do all three of the following:

1) Interact with other members of our species.

2) Plan and organize their time. (I have two hours of homework to do; I promised my parents I'd help cook dinner.)

3) Eat their own French fries.

What can your 14-year-old son do? Can he ride his bike to the market, buy a bag of groceries, and cook a healthy, inexpensive meal for the family?

What can your 16-year-old son do? Can he mow the lawn? Can he plan, design, organize, and follow through on a long-term project? Can he do his own laundry? Can he walk the dog, bathe the dog, take the dog to the vet? Can he find his way across town using public transportation? Can he use the Internet to make a plane reservation and pay for it? Can he dress appropriately and show up on time for a job interview? Can he get up in the morning by himself and get to school on time?

***

Tell me if the following rings true: "Davy? Davy! Get up! Get out of bed, would you please? It's noon for crying out loud. Davy, do you hear me? Get out of bed. Here, let me help you with your shoes. Now go out there and kill a b'ar. How many times do I have to tell you?"

"And for goodness gracious sake, put down that video game!"

45

"Mother, I'd rather do it myself!" shouted a woman on a headache *commercial. Did you ever wonder what she was so upset about?*

Can You Shut Up?

"Can you shut up?" doesn't actually mean "Can you shut up?" "Can you shut up?" means "Will you shut up?" Because presumably, the speaker is physiologically capable of shutting up—unless there is some new disease ("foot in mouth"?)—of which I am unaware. The question is whether or not the speaker will stop talking.

Just as many adults are tired of being harangued by newscasters, salespeople, advertisements, and other kinds of incessant stimulus overload, many of our children have had it up to here with the sound of parental voices. Imagine a world—a more silent world—where children were sometimes left alone to figure it out for themselves. Would you be able to leave them alone?

"That stick is too big! Put more twigs over here! There isn't enough room there for air to get in!"

That's one way to teach your nine-year-old son how to build a campfire. But it makes me nervous just thinking about all those words out in the woods. Another way to teach your nine-year-old son to build a campfire would be to say, "There's a fire pit and some twigs."

"But if I don't tell him how to do things, how will he ever learn?"

You are not the be all and end all of information. Your children are learning a great deal—much of the information we'd be happy for them not to have—without you, their parents. You didn't teach them about Taylor Swift or Facebook. You didn't teach them how to play "Blood, Blood, Blood, Shoot, Shoot, Shoot, Kill, Kill, Kill."

The question is whether or not you're going to have the kind of relationship with your kids where they are open to hearing about what's important. Because they haven't been inundated with endless verbiage from the time they were old enough to hear.

"In a relationship," teaches one of my favorite therapists, "repeating something more than three times in a year is nagging."

How can we expect our kids to distinguish what is important—"Don't take drugs"—from what they need to figure out for themselves: whether or not they want to take music lessons, how to entertain themselves (without screens!), what clothes to wear? If we just keep up the constant stream of words, how will they figure out that they are capable of figuring things out?

I know a sophomore in college who lives in a dorm in the town where she grew up. She takes a full course load and is on the crew team. When she gets back to her room after classes and athletic practice, she frequently takes a nap.

Or tries to.

Her mother, just as frequently, comes over to her daughter's dorm room and wakes her up. "Do your homework" she exclaims. "You have a paper due!"

166

"Why can't you get organized like your older sisters? Don't you know how important your college grades are?"

You know who else—after the age of four—doesn't get to decide when to sleep and when to study? Prisoners of war.

If your high school-aged child isn't getting out of bed, getting dressed on her own, and getting to school on time, then there's something wrong. But here again, yelling at her isn't going to solve the problem and may make the situation worse. The relevant questions might have more to do with WHY the kid isn't willing or able to get herself together and get to school.

When your preschooler is trying to do a puzzle, let him alone. If you do the puzzle for him, you will communicate that getting the puzzle done is more important to you than your child enjoying the process. Emphasis on completion is not what the child is about. If mom's anxiety is causing her to complete the puzzle for the child, mom should back off.

If your elementary school child is making brownies, let him alone (until it's time to work together to clean up the kitchen.) If the goal of the process were to have some brownies, you could go to the market and buy some. What we're looking at here is a child figuring it out. And who knows, along the way he may learn how many cups are in an ounce.

Science Fair projects, needless to say, should be done by middle schoolers, not by their parents. "But all the other families are cheating" is a poor argument. It's middle school for goodness gracious sake! No one cares. I've been working in college admissions for over three decades. Here are words I have never heard: "Well, Johnny looked like a viable candidate here at Olde Brick University, but then we found out that he didn't win the science fair in seventh grade!"

College application essays should be written by the applicant. College application essays written by parents are 1) easily detected by my colleagues in admissions, and 2) subvert the integrity of the student's process. "We love you and trust you and are sending you off to college, but we're writing your essays for you"? Bad plan.

Just as our children need silence from screens so that they can reflect, look inward and—imagine!—think about picking up a book, they also need a

167

break from the constant advice that gushes from well-meaning parents. By "picking our battles" and focusing on what our kids need rather on what we want to tell them, we increase the odds that they will grow up to be able to make good decisions on their own.

46

Although the following gentle advice is directed toward our college-aged children rather than their parents, I'm hopeful that moms and dads can still put it to good use. How do we help our kids be the people who are willing to get out there and DO something? Answer: by encouraging our kids to take appropriate risks and by modeling the behavior that it's okay to try and fail.

What Good is Sitting Alone in your Room?

Next week, there's a 50-kilometer race in Connecticut. A hundred of my new best friends (whom I'll likely never see again) as well as a few of the gang I've been running with for years are going to head up to Danbury, hurl ourselves into the void, and give it a try. What the heck? Why not? How hard could it be? Running 50-K is just like running 5-K only we get to do it ten times instead of just once.

The point is, you never know what will happen when you get out there and do something.

I have another friend who will not be joining us. "The outdoors is my second favorite place," he suggests. "I'll be thinking of you as I finish my second cup of freshly brewed, exquisite coffee and read the New York Times in the privacy of my air-conditioned living room. I may commemorate your hitting the 20-mile mark by taking a nap."

I'm sensitive to the "all the comforts of home" view, but there are any number of reasons for running 31 miles. What is most cogent for me is epitomized by one of my grandmother's favorite sayings: "You're a long time dead." Or as the songwriter put it:

Start by admitting
From cradle to tomb
Isn't that long a stay.
Life is a cabaret, old chum
Only a cabaret.

Some of my college students seem oblivious to the thunder in the word "hour" in "Life's but a walking shadow, a poor player / That struts and frets his hour upon the stage / And then is heard no more." And who could blame them? At 18, they have their whole lives ahead of them; anything is possible; what difference could it make if they stay in their dorm rooms? Indeed, if they're truly content playing "Shoot, Shoot, Shoot, Blood, Blood, Blood, Kill, Kill, Kill" and seldom interacting with actual humans, who am I to say that there is a whole world out there that might be more fulfilling? Who am I to throw a stone?

Speaking of stones, this morning, I nearly tripped over one (might have been a root—it's impossible to see at 5:45 in the morning) and almost did a face plant on a trail in the park. Am I advocating for falling over and injuring myself rather than staying safely inside a home with—presumably—fewer rocks and roots?

Certainly not. I'm just in favor of getting out there and doing something.

Truly, it's better to be on the ground wishing you were up in an airplane than it is to be in an airplane wishing you were on the ground.

But at the same time, if you're lonely, wishing for friends, hoping there would

170

be more to the college experience than going to class and lumping around in your dorm room then it might be time to make a change. Get up. Get out.

Do I have a specific suggestion? Of course it depends on the individual and every college has dozens of viable options, but why not join the newspaper staff?

"Yes, but there are no girls I like on the newspaper. They're a bunch of literary types. I'm more of the outdoorsy type."

"Okay, then join the outdoors club."

"Yes, but it's too cold in the winter here to do much outdoors."

"Then join the newspaper staff, darn it. If you don't like writing, sell advertisements or do the books or sweep the floor. There's always something to do. And most importantly, even if there are no girls you like, something will happen, something good, something to tell a story about years later, something. Just get out there."

"Yes, but I just said that I don't like any of those girls."

"Maybe those girls know some other girls. I don't know. What I do know is that if you're sitting by yourself in your dorm room playing "Shoot, Shoot, Shoot, Blood, Blood, Blood, Kill, Kill, Kill" then the likelihood of a girl knocking on your door is pretty close to zero."

The run this morning was about as plebian as could be, nothing much to talk about with the same group of friends with whom I've been running for the past several decades. We see each other several times a week for the treks through the dark. "Family okay?" "Yeah, everything's good. You?" "Taking my son to the dentist later. Just a cleaning. How's work?" "Same old. Lots to do." "Talk to Lorna?" "Yeah, she ran yesterday, won't be here until later."

We run through the parking lot at Tropical Park just as we've done every Tuesday morning since Regan was president. Not much to say. The same group of middle aged, paunchy, balding men trying to stave off the inevitable one mile and one Tuesday morning at a time. Big picture items—"staying healthy is the greatest gift you can give to the people who care about you"—

are lost in the early morning ebb and flow of gentle (another word would be "boring") conversation.

When suddenly, from out of nowhere, a flock of ibis—two dozen birds strong—appears from the east. They do a synchronized swoop, flying within 30 feet of us, squawking like a herd of staple guns. They loop around us, their motion magnificent. For all the thousands of early-morning miles that Bruce, Daniel, and I have run together, we are overwhelmed at how perfectly harmonious these birds are. It is hard to imagine that they don't get together "after school" for flying practice. They circle us once again as if showing off and—as suddenly as they appeared—are gone.

Had we been sitting alone in our rooms, this most magnificent spectacle would have gone unnoticed.

My gentle advice for first year college students and for everyone else: get out there. Do something.

I'll let you know how the 31 miles goes. I'm guessing—whether or not there are flocks of ibis coming out of the sun in Connecticut—that there are going to be some outrageous stories.

In so many endeavors, it is important to be right, to stick to your guns. In conversations with our children, it is frequently more important to shut up, not just so they can figure things out for themselves, but also so that they can feel valued rather than harangued.

How Do You Win at Chicken?

Not, how do you win a chicken? I can only assume that there are any number of country fairs across our great nation that allow you to put down your cotton candy, pick up a baseball, and win a chicken. Referenced here is the "game" of chicken involving two cars, two drivers, and one (hopefully) deserted stretch of highway.

The participants—leather-clad teenagers with a predilection for all things mechanical and a thriving distrust for adults—speed toward one another in their hotrods. As the speed of both cars approaches 80 miles per hour, the distance between them decreases at the rate of 23 feet every tenth of a second. Whichever driver turns away first loses—is the "chicken."

What is the winning strategy for this admittedly stupid but all too real game?

Obviously, staying out of either car would be your best bet. Being elsewhere, almost anywhere elsewhere, is highly recommended. But assuming, for the sake of this essay, that you are the driver of a car hurtling down a road at warp speed, what is your best strategy? How do you win? How do you convince the other driver to turn off before you smack into one another at a combined velocity of 160 miles per hours and become scattered body parts?

If I'm not mistaken, it was Nixon's Secretary of State, Henry Kissinger, who first posed this situation and its solution back in the cold war days. But my column this week is about when it's wrong to be right, not about geo-political brinksmanship.

First, some examples of when I am right: as an independent college admissions counselor with 30 years of experience, I know when a student will be happier at a big state university as opposed to a private liberal arts college. As a safe driver, I am always in the right. All the rest of the drivers in Miami are either psychopaths or visually-challenged.* The question is how to convey my "rightness" to those who would benefit from my insight. How do I communicate to a 17-year-old with learning differences and modest academic motivation that she will be lost and overwhelmed at a mega-versity with 400 students in freshman biology? And how do I convince all those other drivers that I have the right of way? The two situations may have more in common than it would seem at first. My being right may not be the most important part of the conversation.

Here's an activity in which it is important to be right: building jet engines.

Here's where it's important to let it go: divorce proceedings. Raising kids. College counseling. Driving.

Here's my rule of thumb about being right: if it has a thumb, it's not so important to be right.

174

Machines don't have thumbs. They have to be built to exact specifications with prescribed limitations of error. Kids do have thumbs. Let them win an argument once in a while.

Remember that great ad for safe driving from years ago? The narrator walks through the wreckage of a brutal car accident—shards of glass, twisted metal—and says, "This guy was right." He kicks a piece of a shattered bumper. "Dead right."

Kids who get yelled at all the time—"Do your homework;" "Change your clothes;" "Your friends are idiots"—won't remember the specifics, only that they are always in the wrong. Your disapproval will be remembered more than your guidance.

The paradigm for raising kids is not a game of chicken.

* For the chronically irony impaired, let me state explicitly that I am kidding about the above examples.

48

Here is another thought about how to bring up healthy kids. Again, there is no definitive answer nor guarantee, but hanging out with your kids just for the fun of it a hundred miles from the nearest homework worksheet may be part of the solution.

Bear with Me

Better writers than I have tried to describe that truly torrential, bone-drenching, incessant rain storm where the water comes down in sheets, shows no signs of abating, and has soaked you through the skin going back generations. Not seeing any of these writers at a campsite on top of Stone Mountain in North Georgia, my nine-year-old son and I made the sensible determination that we could eat sandwiches for dinner, in that an hour and a half of trying to build a fire with wet wood seemed like more than enough. The fire would not start even when we "cheated" and used paper. Without a fire, we could throw the leftovers into the darkness where the woodland creatures, now lining up two by two, could eat them.

Fortunately, we had two good books and extra flashlight batteries so we felt good about our ability to get through the night even if we were unable to sleep much because of the thunder. Unfortunately, we had left the flaps of the tent open, so there was an inch and a half of water on the floor. It has been said that discretion is the better part of valor. I don't know what the better part of common sense is, but I was pleased when Ellery suggested that many parts of the inside of the car were somewhat dry and that we could sleep there. This we proceeded to do, noting appreciatively how beautiful the woods must have been—not that we could see any trees through the rain.

As can well be imagined, our trip was subject to a little scrutiny and a lot of ridicule when we got back to dry land:

"But what do you do on these trips?" one friend asked. "Even if I could understand why a middle-aged man with a bad back would want to sleep on rocks and roots without electricity and have to walk a hundred yards though a deluge to get to a bathroom that hasn't been updated since the Truman administration, what do you talk about?"

When I didn't have a response, he continued with even more sarcasm: "No wait, I get it. You say, 'Look, son. That's a cow.' And he says, 'Thanks, Dad!'"

Maybe because my ears were still filled with water, I couldn't come up with a response to justify why I had spent my vacation in a swamp on top of a mountain eating damp PBJs.

"Car camping?" He continued. "Isn't that a lot like *motel* camping?"

***

This time I did have a rejoinder. "Certainly not," I explained. "The sun came out the next day and my son and I took a walk."

"Isn't that called a *hike?*"

I saw no reason to mention that we hadn't gotten a hundred yards from the tent before I slipped in some calf-deep mud, twisted my ankle, and had to spend the rest of the day limping around the campsite using inappropriate language.

So, instead I said, "Besides, there are animals in the woods. You never know when you'll see a red-shouldered hawk or a fox. And there have been black bear sightings in the area close to where we were."

"Dad, we didn't see an animal bigger than a mosquito," my son pointed out.

I pointed out that my son should go put away the camping gear.

Then I said goodbye to my friend and sat down with my son to start planning the next trip.

***

Many times, the reason to do things with your kids is so that you'll have a good story to tell afterwards. Remember the time we went hiking at Gunpowder Falls and we had walked around all afternoon and couldn't find the falls and we asked the ranger why the park was called Gunpowder Falls if there weren't any falls and the ranger said, "We get asked that a lot"?

Which is not to say that going camping with your kids is the only way to bring up happy, healthy, content, self-actualized kids who pass the bar exam the first time and happily communicate with their parents in their old age. I see lots of families who go camping where the generations have poor relationships. I see lots of families who never set foot outdoors who get along beautifully. I would only suggest that the groundwork for communication is unlikely to be productively laid out if the only conversations in the home revolve around arguments about doing homework.

The metaphors have to come from somewhere. And I have come to believe that the only real learning comes from metaphors. When your kids face the inevitable disappointments—a failed driving test, a disappointing exam result, a called third strike, a refused marriage proposal—isn't it great to be able to put the experience in context? Aren't you pleased when there is a prior experience on which to base the hope of going forward?

Wordsworth may have defined poetry as the "spontaneous overflow of powerful emotions recollected in tranquility" but couldn't he have just as easily been talking about our relationships with our children?

178

"Remember that clear April morning when we left the campsite before dawn and walked to the top of the mountain where the sun burst through and lit up the valley and we could see for miles and we saw that hawk come out of the west and fly over the trees like it was showing off just for us?"

How many nights would you be willing to sleep in a wet car to have one memory like that one on which to look back?

49

What if you can't have it all? What if your expectations for how your life would be with children turn out to be overly optimistic? Are you going to be stuck with your disappointments or can you compromise?

Let's Make a Deal

Here's a joke from 40 years ago. Let me know if you recognize it:

A man comes home from work to see his two-year-old son on the kitchen floor happily playing in a puddle of spilled milk. In the next room, the man observes his older son, age five, shaving the cat with an electric razor. Walking gingerly past dirty laundry and piles of dishes, the man heads upstairs through a maze of toys strewn over each step.

In the bedroom, he sees his wife sprawled happily in her housedress with her feet up, eating chocolates, watching television. Outraged, the man sputters: "What the heck is going on here?"

His wife calmly replies, "Remember yesterday when you asked me what I do here all day? Well, today, I didn't do it."

Which brings us to a more serious point: what if it turns out that you can't have it all?

What if—when your children are aged five, three, and one—you can have a clean house or a happy house, but not both? Obviously, we would all prefer—in a perfect world—to live in a house that is both tidy and one in which there is sweetness and light. Obviously we would prefer good conversation and loving relationships to walk hand in hand with order and cleanliness. Clearly, a five-year-old should not be shaving the cat with a razor, electric or otherwise. But what if it's just not possible? What if the only way to have a clean house is for mom and dad to clean for hours after working and taking care of children all day? What if by cleaning until all hours, they are so grouchy that they fuss at one another and the children?

What if the solution is to let the dishes pile up in the sink all day? Who could bear to live with such a mess? If the only way to have a clean house is to have a home where the grown-ups are miserable, maybe a slight move in the direction of disorder may be the way to go.

***

What if your child refuses to play the didgeridoo?

In an ideal world, your gentle protestations would encourage her to love music in general and the didgeridoo specifically. She would look forward to practicing the didgeridoo; she would invite her friends over for didgeridoo quartets. But down here in this world inhabited by actual children, didgeridoo practice has become a power and control issue that escalates to the point of nuclear war.

Of course, you can force her to practice the didgeridoo. You are the parent after all and have the power to enforce your will. You can threaten and coerce, punish and reward, bully and bribe.

But at what cost? At some point, a happy home without the dulcet sounds of the didgeridoo may be preferable to a miserable one with an accomplished didgeridoo player.

***

Here's the toughest argument of all: maybe your child is not going to get a PhD in philosophy from Princeton. Even if you give her psycho-stimulants.

Is your ninth grader studying six hours a day, more on the weekends? If he is doing endless homework, filling in worksheets, memorizing tedious information? Are you at war, every day of the school year? Is your child prevaricating with you because every conversation about schoolwork becomes a war? Is your child so nervous before tests that he has stomach trouble and so nervous before exams that he throws up?

Maybe it's time to think about reorganizing the priorities of the family.

When your wife said, "It's time" and you drove like a stunt driver to the hospital, you wanted two things: to get to the delivery room on time and to have a baby with ten fingers and ten toes.

That was the deal and you promised your higher power, "God, just give me a healthy baby and I'll never ask for anything ever again. All I want is to see ten fingers and ten toes."

And when—some anxiety laden hours later—you held your healthy son in your arms and you wept for joy and you stroked your wife's hair and you knew that never in your life could you ever be so relieved and happy again, was there any conversation about a didgeridoo?

I didn't think so.

If I could ensure that my child would be happy and healthy, productive and content, I'd be willing to consider making him clean the house, play the didgeridoo, and take Adderall for his attentional issues. If instead all I can guarantee is that we'll all be grumpy with each other if I force him to do these things, I'm going to go back to being grateful that he has ten fingers and toes.

50

There are few cogent sentences about parenting that make sensible use of the phrases "It is always imperative to..." or "It is never okay to..." Just the same, I'm going to go out on a limb here and suggest that you kill your screens.

Reading Fried Chicken

Everyone wants to eat in a health food restaurant, right? Because eating in a health food restaurant is, well, healthy. As a matter of fact, you can't spell "Health Food Restaurant" without the word "Health" and it says "Health Food Restaurant" in big letters right there over the door.

The menu is replete with healthy choices—low carb, no sugar, gluten-free, and whole grain. Vegetables abound. Eating this stuff is how you get healthy, lose weight, feel good about your diet, feel good about yourself. Eating at a health food restaurant is the first step in living a healthy life. By eating quinoa I can stave off heart disease and boost my immune system. What could be better?

Of course there, at the bottom of the menu, is one more entree. Listed last, after the tofu, veggie burger, seitan, carrots, and quinoa are two words: "fried" and "chicken."

And that's what pretty much everybody orders.

Owners of health food restaurants know what their customers order. They tally up the meals at the end of the shift:

Wheat Grass: 1
Whole Grain Smoothie: 1
Avocado and Purified Sawdust: 1
Fried Chicken: 978

Whoever said, "Eating healthy doesn't make you live longer, it just feels that way" was ordering the fried chicken for sure.

At the library, the same thing happens. No, the children aren't eating brussel sprouts in the stacks. The children are ignoring books of all kinds in favor of computers. *A Wrinkle in Time; To Kill a Mockingbird; Island of the Blue Dolphins; Ramona Quimby, Age 8; The Phantom Tollbooth*; and *Old Yeller* all wait patiently on the shelves while children sign on to Facebook, "just for a minute." Putting computers in a library makes as much sense as having an open bar at an AA meeting.

And don't tell me that the kids are on the computers reading interactive novels, because they're not. I did extensive, methodologically-precise, sophisticated research on the subject of "computer usage in public libraries" (read: I took my kids to the library the other day and looked around.) The children on the computers were "reading" in the same sense that picking your nose is "exercising."

The kids on the computers weren't deeply engrosses in a novel art form. They were drowning in social media.

Unless, of course, they were playing "Shoot, Shoot, Shoot, Blood, Blood, Blood, Kill, Kill, Kill."

It's one thing to pay $600 for a one-year gym membership. It's something else

184

entirely to get up early, five days a week, rain or shine, and get your sorry butt onto those treacherous weight machines last used in the Spanish Inquisition. Going to church doesn't make you a Christian any more than sleeping in a garage makes you a car. Going to the library is the first step; actually reading books is another.

How do we encourage our children to love to read? Follow this simple two-step plan:

1) Model reading. Get off your own darn computer and read a book. You heard it here first.

2) Unplug all your screens—TV, computer games, video of all kinds.

But wait! There's more! Here's a bonus suggestion absolutely free!

3) When your child comes home with an insipid worksheet—"read this colorless paragraph then answer these picayune questions,"—a paper seemingly designed to lessen your child's potential loving relationship with the written word, just say no! Tell your kid not to spend time on the homework; instead, tell her to read a book.

What were your favorite books as an adolescent? Would you have read as much if the alternative was to play "Shoot, Shoot, Shoot, Blood, Blood, Blood, Kill, Kill, Kill" seven hours a day?

"Love the children you have and you'll have the children you'll love" could
have been the name of this book. This fundamental expression of the joy of
being a parent is too often lost as we foolishly teach our kids to compete and
to focus on "being the best." Instead, we should value, accept, and love them
for who they are.

Stumpers

Here's a riddle you may enjoy: what do Winnie the Pooh and Atilla the Hun
have in common?*

In the meantime, the following hint from Groucho Marx may be of help: "A
child of five would understand this. Send someone to fetch a child of five." In
other words, young ones may have more luck with this riddle than do their
parents.

Here's an even more difficult question, the answer to which neither

186

generation will find obvious at first blush. What do the following stories and movies all have in common?

1) "The Town Mouse and the Country Mouse," the fable by Aesop.

2) "The Sorcerer's Apprentice." (Go ahead, think about Mickey Mouse in Fantasia. Disney got the idea from Goethe's 1797 story.)

3) The Wonderful Wizard of Oz, by L. Frank Baum. (Again, full marks if you think about the 1939 MGM movie rather than the less well-known book.)

4) "The Monkey's Paw," an admittedly obscure but none-the-less wonderful 1906 horror story by W. W. Jacobs.

And for those who don't have the time or inclination to reread, rewatch, or rethink, here are the relevant passages:

1) From Aesop: "Better beans and bacon in peace than cakes and ale in fear."

2) From Goethe: "Spirits that I've cited, My commands ignore." (Or if you're thinking Fantasia, envision Mickey splitting the brooms in half, but more and more brooms keep bringing water. He has started a process that he does not have the skill to contain.)

3) From The Wonderful Wizard of Oz, "My greatest wish now," [Dorothy] added, "is to get back to Kansas..."

4) From "The Monkey's Paw," the parents of the maimed and mangled son just want their old lives back.

Why are there so many stories across generations, across centuries, across countries and cultures about wishing for changes that ultimately make things worse rather than better? From Aesop 2,500 years ago in Greece to late 18th century Germany to Depression Era Kansas to a hundred years ago in Britain, all these stories seem to be asking, "Could we wish for something better?" and the resounding answer is: "Not so much."

If the morals of the story are "stay as you are" and "don't wish for change," then, it could be argued, the ruling elite propagate these myths. The king

187

doesn't want anyone other than his son applying for the job of imperial ruler. If everyone from mice to apprentices to farm girls to working class Englishmen are encouraged to accept the status quo and stay in their social class, there is less work to be done quelling insurrection. But that's not how I read these stories.

The message that I get is two-fold. Firstly, change—transformative positive change—is incremental. Hard work pays off in a better life for your children. Big changes—oxycontin for mild pain, for example—have long term, negative consequences. Secondly—and here regular readers will sense another familiar theme—being satisfied with the children we have will lead us to not muck things up by trying to force them to be the children they're not. Because the law of unintended consequences can destroy our families.

"Jill wasn't doing well in math, so I went in and yelled at her teacher. I was shocked to learn that now my daughter expects me to solve all her problems and is unable to do much for herself."

"Micah wanted to study music, but I insisted that he put away his instrument and focus on chemistry. Now I'm disappointed that he doesn't trust my judgment."

"Jason wasn't studying as much as I would have liked, so I gave him psycho-stimulants for attention. Then I was surprised when he started taking Xanax believing he could cure every unhappiness with a pill."

"Tommy wanted to go to bed after studying for four hours, but I slapped him and said that if he wanted to achieve his goals, he would have to study for five hours. I just can't understand why now, as an adult, he won't return my calls."

I am not advocating for mediocrity. I am not suggesting that we discourage our children from trying that which is new, healthy, and appropriate. I am arguing that trying to change children into who we want them to be can have unintended and dire results. As always, love the kids you have and you'll have the kids you'll love. After all, wouldn't you rather have a child who is studying to be a sorcerer than a mouse who is surrounded by too many brooms with overflowing buckets of water?

*Winnie the Pooh and Atilla the Hun have the same middle name.

52

So many parents complain of the ingratitude of their children. How do we give our children the gift of allowing them to make a contribution? Not by refusing to allow them to do anything for themselves or for our families.

What Have You Done for Me Next?

"You were working as a waitress in a cocktail bar,
When I met you.
I picked you out, I shook you up, and turned you around; turned you into someone new.
Now five years later on you've got the world at your feet, Success has been so easy for you.
But don't forget it's me who put you where you are now, and I can put you back down too."

Needless to say, by the end of the song, it is clear that she has dumped him.

***

Twenty-seven years and three grown children into his marriage, Mr. Thompson develops aplastic anemia which only an allogenic bone marrow transplant can cure. Miraculously, his wife is a match. She donates and Mr. Thompson has a rapid, remarkable, and relatively painless recovery.

On the day that the doctor tells the Thompsons that Mr. Thompson doesn't even need to make a subsequent appointment—that he is as healthy as the proverbial ox, that his cancer is in complete and total remission—Mr. Thompson files for divorce.

***

Simon works full time at the post office, a soul-denying job he detests. He is a good father to his three children and a devoted husband to his wife. Toward the end of her life, Simon's mother-in-law comes to live with him. As her dementia increases, she becomes an increasing burden, both emotional and economic, but Simon never complains. His days off from his civil service job are filled with doctor visits and care for his mother-in-law. In the fullness of time, Simon's mother-in-law passes away—three years after she moved in. Simon's wife never thanks him for his sacrifice.

***

In one of my favorite Mark Twain short stories, three men are trapped in a blizzard with no hope of surviving the night of unrelenting cold. Believing themselves to be miles from shelter, devoid of food, fuel, or provisions, they huddle around their dwindling campfire as the temperature continues to plummet and talk about what they would have done differently and how they would mend their ways in the future. Each agreed he would have been a better husband and father, would have gone to church more, donated time and money to the poor. All agree that, were they to be delivered, they would never drink again. For emphasis, one man hurls his pipe into the darkness, vowing that were he to somehow survive the raging storm, he would never stoop to the vice of smoking tobacco again.

Contrary to the laws of nature, the snow stops. The morning sun reveals that the happy band of travelers is stranded not in a remote and desolate spot but half a mile from a village.

The man walks over, picks up his pipe, and heads on into town.

***

You and your new business associate go out to lunch. When the check comes, you reach for it and exclaim, "I'll get this one." Some people understand that the precedent is that you will take turns paying for meals. On the other hand, some people perceive that they never have to get a check.

***

Where does all the gratitude go? How does a man who has just accepted a bone marrow transplant leave his wife? How does a woman whose husband has taken his mother-in-law into his home not feel thankful? How does a man who has been saved from certain frozen death not keep his promise? How can a man for whom you have picked up a lunch check not take his turn?

The parents with whom I work frequently have "picked up all the checks" for their children. By doing so, they deny their children the opportunity to give back, to feel good about themselves, to make a contribution to the family. Children should be ALLOWED to do their own laundry, to weed the garden, to walk the dog, to set the table, to clean the pool. Nobody but a prostitute wants to be paid for all the time.

A child who is given a hundred dollars on the first Friday of the month will be less happy than a child who earns ten dollars the first Friday, twenty dollars the second, thirty dollars the third and forty dollars on the fourth Friday. Both children have a hundred dollars in total. But earning is better than getting, and four payouts are better than one. The first child will be happy only briefly.

How do we allow our adolescent children to be happy and content? How do we allow them to move in the direction of being self-actualized?

Not by doing everything for them.

53

It's easy to root for a winner; it's easy to love the successful kids. But what about the children for whom nothing comes easy?

The Other Side of the Street

As a baby, Nero was easy to soothe. Within a few weeks of coming home from the hospital, he slept through the night. All his developmental milestones were within normal limits—talking, walking, potty training. Nero learned to dress himself, ride a bike, read a book, and make a sandwich just when he was supposed to. His parents could not have been more pleased. Mr. and Mrs. Typicale felt that their responsibilities as parents were modest. "The child practically raises himself," they were fond of saying. "We feel like we're just along for the ride."

Now in high school, Nero seldom studies more than two hours a day; he doesn't have to. He takes sparse notes, writing down only the few concepts that he doesn't understand. These ideas, which are almost always the very ones he needs to know for the test, he quickly absorbs and remembers using his aptitude and good memory. His junior year courses—Advanced Placement English, Advanced Placement History, Advanced Placement Calculus, Advanced Placement Chemistry, Spanish IV, and Ceramics (there is a fine arts requirement at his private school)—come easily to him. Although he is well liked and respected by his classmates, he does not attend the parties with 200 kids. He has a few close friends with whom he plays sports on the weekends.

Which is not to say that Nero hasn't had a few bumps along the way. After working at a camp last summer, he attended a party. One of the older kids offered Nero a cup of beer, which he drank. Of course, the adults found out and Nero got in trouble. He was ordered to do community service hours—which he performed cheerfully—and he will not be allowed to work at the camp ever again.

In the year since "the incident," Nero hasn't gone near alcohol. Indeed, he frequently declines invitations to social gatherings: "You know what goes on there," he explains. Instead, he gets together with "the boring kids," as he calls them. "You know," he goes on, "the ones who have a future." In short, Nero is a "one-time learner." His mistakes make him sharper, and he doesn't repeat them.

***

Difficult from the day he was born, Dane was colicky, a poor sleeper, hard to soothe, and harder to parent. Neither the pediatrician, the pre-school teacher, nor the school psychologist could quite explain why Dane behaved the way he did or what his parents should do about it. "He picks up on your nervousness; that's why he doesn't sleep," a helpful neighbor explained. "If we could get any sleep, we wouldn't be so nervous," Dane's mother rejoined.

As the years went on, Mrs. Bramage's troubles only increased: Dane had poor grades, a poor attitude toward school, learning differences, attentional issues, poor social skills, and low self-esteem. Dane's parents took him to every specialist. Some were more sensitive than others; none were helpful.

As a high school student, Dane doesn't seem to learn from his mistakes. He got caught for underage drinking, but was drinking again within a month. He doesn't study for his exams, so he does poorly; but doesn't study for the next

193

test either. "He just doesn't get it," his parents lament. "We don't know what to do."

***

Imagine what it's like to be Nero. Everything comes easily—academics, athletics, social interactions. Sure, he works hard, but he gets the job done. When he studies, he gets an A. When he asks out a girl, she usually says 'OK.' And when a girl turns him down or he gets a C on a calculus test, or he loses a close game, the message he hears in his head is "I'll work a little harder next time and do a little better." Because he has the skills, ability, and background to do so, he doesn't take his minor defeats to heart.

Now imagine what it's like to be Dane. It doesn't seem to matter how much he studies, his results are always similar. He doesn't see the relationship between hard work and success because, for him, there is no relationship between hard work and success. He memorizes the locations and spellings of the countries in Africa and the next morning he has little recognition. He reads *The Great Gatsby*, but doesn't understand or remember what he has read.

The social piece is worse than the academic: in the rare instance when he does get up the courage to ask a girl on a date, she turns him down and he doesn't even understand exactly what she has said. "I'd love to, but I have plans that night." What does that mean? Would she love to? Does she actually have plans? Or are those statements polite lies? How is he supposed to know?
Dane's teachers yell at him or, at best, ignore him. The disappointment of his parents is palpable. He has few friends.

***

Next time you're feeling smug about what wonderful children you have, about how they're doing well, achieving their goals, succeeding, and making you proud, take a moment to reflect on how much of their ability is attributable to you and how much to blind chance. You took your daughter to the library when she was little? Good for you.

But so did Dane's parents.

194

Not all of how great your kids are can be traced back to your patience, guidance, insight, and brilliance. Some of it was dumb luck.

Reflect on King Lear, homeless in the storm, thinking about how he might have been more sympathetic to those who weren't born in a palace:

Poor naked wretches, wheresoever you are,
That bide the pelting of this pitiless storm,
How shall your houseless heads and unfed sides,
Your looped and windowed raggedness, defend you
From seasons such as these? O, I have taken
Too little care of this!

Lastly, and as always, I exhort you to love the kids you have and you'll get the kids you'll love. I can't help but wonder: if Lear had loved Cordelia for who she was rather than for what she said, maybe a great tragedy could have been averted.

***

(Did anyone notice that Nero Typicale is as close as I could come to "Neurotypical" and Dane Bramage is my approximation of "Brain Damaged"?)

54

Striving to be the best is stupid. Emphasis on winning makes losers of all our children. There. I've said it and I'm glad.

You Miss All the Shots You Don't Take

I want to take this opportunity to talk about a player with whom I shared a season in the sun on an intramural softball team a scant three and a half decades ago. I may have forgotten every theorem from my Non-Euclidean Geometry and Convexity course from about the same epoch, but I remember vividly our human vacuum cleaner of a short stop. He was a black hole on the infield, through which no ball could penetrate. He could move to his right; he seemed to hover parallel to the ground absorbing hard hit balls. He could leap half his body length into the air stealing base hits. Watching him from my position in left field was a joy.

He was so good, so extraordinarily good. He was such a natural athlete...

196

...that he never even got a tryout for a division three college team.

Never mind a shot at a professional minor league team.

It's a steep pyramid in the world of grown-up sports. There are several hundred major league baseball players in a country of several hundred million people. To say nothing of the Dominican Republic, Japan, and other climes where many young people dream of playing under the lights as adults.

I wonder, all these years later, if our short stop was happy with his ability. He was far and away the best the player on our team. He would have been the worst player by far on any real college team. Was he satisfied? Was he pleased with his ability?

Or did he spend his whole life thinking about what could have been had his skills been even better? Did he spend years fixated on "if only"?

Because if the only way he could have been happy was to be the best ever, his odds of being happy were slender indeed. If he could be happy knowing he had given it his best shot, then his odds of contentment were significantly higher.

Stated more grammatically: all this emphasis on excellence leaves me cold. All this talk about being the best makes me ill.

Because, by definition, only one person can be the best. What's the point of all that striving if all you care about is winning?

Is Willie Mays a loser because he has "only" 660 lifetime home runs? At fifth on the all-time list, he's not the "best ever."

One of my favorite athletes ran a 18:52 for five kilometers in the last race of his senior year of high school. He took the event seriously and ran hard; he had trained hard for four years. He threw up at mile two, but didn't slow down.

Had he been enrolled at a high school across town, his time of 18:52 would have been the best performance at the 5K distance in the 50-year history of that institution. His name would have been printed in big letters on the "All

197

Time Best" placard outside the gym. At his school, on the other hand, 18:52 wasn't good enough to put him in the top seven runners on that day.

If this athlete were concerned with winning, he would have nothing to celebrate. Because he was concerned with "only" doing the best he could, he has a memory for a lifetime: he ran faster than he ever had before; he ran so hard he puked; he didn't quit.

If he defines winning narrowly as beating Kenenisa Bekele's world record time of 12:37, he'll have a lifetime of disappointment. It seems unlikely that the high school kid would knock off two minutes per mile from his best.

The take away for parents is obvious: stop focusing on grades, stop emphasizing norm referenced test scores, stop convincing your school children that they can only win if someone else loses. At the risk of sounding like Pogo the Possum: the only person to whom they can compare themselves is them.

Imagine a class where the requirements are as modest as they are meaningless, where students comply rather than learn, where grades are assigned on the basis of posture rather than insight. What does an 'A' in this class mean? Imagine to the contrary, a class where students learn to love reading and talking about literature. The skills and the insights gained from this class might be more important than the letter on the report card.

Here are some easy riddles to make this point:

1) What do you call the person who is graduated last in her medical school class? Answer: Doctor.

2) What do you call the person who is graduated first in her high school class but is stressed and unhappy, unable to learn anything unless she will be tested on the material, and generally miserable? That's right: miserable. (I see a fair number of these students in my practice. It breaks my heart. They know how to win; but they don't know how to live.)

3) What's the point of winning an Olympic medal if, within the next year, the athlete gains a hundred pounds and never runs again? Answer: no point at all.

4) What happened to Kokichi Tsuburaya of Japan who finished third in the 1964 Olympics behind Abebe Bikila and Basil Heatley? (Admittedly, an obscure bit of marathon trivia.) Answer: suicide. The third best distance runner in the world kills himself because he isn't good enough? What's wrong with that picture?

If you'll forgive another running metaphor, here's my new goal: I'm not concerned about winning; I'm not concerned about running faster. I just want to be running at age 70. I want to have nothing left at the end of my life. I want to go out as a wisp of smoke. I don't care if I run faster, I don't care if I run farther. I just want to run until my legs fall off.

And when my legs do fall off from running too many miles over too many years, I'll start in a new category as I pull myself along with my arms.

I suggest you all tell your kids the same thing: try as hard as you can for as long as you can. The heck with the grades; the heck with class rank; the heck with everything except giving it your best shot.

Your children already know what you think. Wouldn't it be worthwhile to learn what they think? How might we go about getting that interesting information?

Silence is Golden

What kind of house do you live in?

1) Are you living with Annie Oakley and Frank Butler (originally played by Ethel Merman and Ray Middleton in the 1946 Broadway musical, "Annie Get Your Gun")? Does your house resound with these lyrics?

"I can do anything you can do better, I can do anything better than you."

Does the chorus,

"No, you can't.

200

Yes, I can.
No, you can't.
Yes, I can.
No, you can't.
Yes, I can,
Yes, I can!"

sound familiar?

Parents frequently tell me about their struggles to get their seventh graders to do homework: "Every night it's the same struggle; we battle over getting the homework done. I am constantly reminding him to do his homework. In the past year, I've told him 100 times to do his homework."

I am tempted to reply: "Then what makes you think that telling him for the 101st time will make any difference?"

It seems more likely that Annie will convince Frank that she is the better shot.
Which isn't going to happen.

2) Wouldn't you rather be living with The Tremeloes*?

"How many times will she fall for his line,
Should I tell her or should I keep cool?
And if I tried, I know she'd say I lied,
Mind your business, don't hurt her, you fool."

***

Yes, it is painful to watch those we love make mistakes. Yes, all loving parents want to step in, say the right words, make the situation better. Wouldn't it be great to be able to solve all the following problems for our beloved children?

1) My son asked a girl to the dance, but she declined his invitation.

Tell him to ask another girl! There are many fish in the sea! There's another streetcar every 20 minutes! Every pot has a lid! She's a stupid girl anyway! Any girl would be lucky to have you!

2) My daughter failed her driver's license test.

Those people at the Department of Motor Vehicles are idiots! I'll have their jobs! How dare they flunk my daughter! I'll show them! You are a good driver!

What about allowing a little golden silence and letting your kids figure things out for themselves? How about just being present for them. Kids get turned down for dates. Kids flunk driver's tests. It happens. Try not to give advice.

Because you can't feel their feeling for them. Because they already know what to do. And by making a lot of noise—no matter what you say—you're just drawing attention to the issue, making it more than it is.

You can be right. But you'll walk alone.

And here's a not so obscure secret: your kids already know what you think.

Take it to the bank. If your child is out of elementary school, she already knows your opinion on every subject you can name. She knows your political opinions; she knows for whom you vote; she knows your thoughts on abortion, gun control, immigration, term limits, the debt ceiling, and whether or not you think the United Nations should intervene in Syria.

Here's another tidbit of information that is not a secret: your 16-year-old son knows whether or not you smoke pot. Why not stand up and communicate in no uncertain terms that in your family, it's not okay to get high? Actions do speak louder than words. You don't have to say anything. Just throw away your stash.

Your kids already know what you think. They may not have gotten the information in the way you think they did. Kids learn by osmosis more than by direct instruction. Next time your kids come to you with a question, rather than responding with a diatribe, why not shrug and say, "I dunno; what do you think?" And then, no matter what they say, just respond, "Sounds like you've given this a lot of thought. I'm sure you'll make the right decision."

One of the best moms I know refuses to speak to her children during carpool. If asked, she'll suggest that she likes to concentrate on her driving. But in reality, she just likes to listen to the kids recounting their perceptions of algebra, recess, and which kids have crushes on each other. Not only do you catch more flies with honey than with vinegar, you get a lot more information from being quiet than from badgering kids with "How was your day?" and "Do you have any homework?"

In short, wake up and smell the information. It's out there.

I'll be quiet now.

* "Silence is Golden" was originally recorded by The Four Seasons in 1964, but was a Number One hit for the Tremeloes, staying at the top of the charts for three weeks in the UK in May of 1967.

56

When my daughter was about seven years old, she asked me one day what I did at work. I told her I worked at the college—that my job was to teach people how to draw. She stared at me, incredulous, and said, "You mean they forget?" ~Howard Ikemoto

They Learn Either Way

When your daughter was four, she wanted to "help" in the kitchen. She wanted to do what you did—break the eggs, follow the recipe, get soap suds on the dishes. Did you let her help or did you get dinner cooked on time? Either way, your daughter learned something: she learned how to crack an egg and she learned that cleaning up a broken egg on the floor is not the end of the world. Alternatively, she learned that it was more important to you to have a meal on time.

When your son was seven, he wanted to follow you around the yard picking up palm fronds. (Note to Northern readers: picking up leaves on steroids is

204

what we do down here rather than shoveling snow.) Did you let him help, even though the job took twice as long? Either way, your son learned something: that any chore can become a game if you have the right attitude. Or he might have learned that getting the yard picked up is more important than having fun with enormous leaves.

When your children were in middle school, did you tell them to do their homework—even when you knew that homework was a series of endlessly repetitive, insipid worksheets seemingly designed to lessen your child's love of reading specifically and more broadly her love of learning altogether? Don't you wish you had played Parcheesi instead?

I am now going to subject my gentle readers—both of you; you know who you are—to a painless math lesson.

Which of the following is more likely to help your children understand simple probability and love learning math?

Column A:

1) A worksheet with rows of 1 + 2, 3 + 5, and 4 + 6 problems arrayed like endless lines of soldiers marching meaninglessly across the page.

2) An equally insipid worksheet about rolling dice: "If you roll two dice, what is the probability of the sum of the dice being seven?*"

Note: Kids who already know what 3 + 5 is will have no trouble doing the worksheets. Kids who don't know what 3 + 5 is will not be able to do the worksheets and won't learn anything. Worksheets of this type are the very definition of "lose/lose."

Column B:

Parcheesi

Rolling dice is intrinsically fun. (Don't believe me? Go to Las Vegas. You'll see adults—lots of them—rolling dice.) A kid who rolls a five and a three will determine what five plus three is with a lot more interest than that same kid doing a worksheet.

Probability is more fun to learn when playing Parcheesi with your family than when doing a worksheet about dice. With any luck at all, your children will learn—after playing enough games of Parcheesi—that going to Las Vegas is a losing proposition. Playing Parcheesi with your kids is "win/win."

Full disclosure: playing Parcheesi with the kids won't get dinner done or the lawn cleaned up. But it may teach them how to add, how to make investment decisions, how to have fun with the family, and how to stay away from gambling.

How do our children ever forget that learning is fun? How do they move on from all those great experiences like helping with dinner, helping in the yard, and playing board games with the family? Teachers and parents tell them to "sit down and shut up." In short, to do work sheets.

Here's an analogy that never appeared on the SAT: doing a math worksheet is to playing Parcheesi with your family as looking at a billboard of two people kissing is to making out with a loved one.

* One out of six. There are six ways to get a seven (1 and 6; 2 and 5; 3 and 4; 4 and 3; 5 and 2; and 6 and 1) out of 36 total possibilities. Six out of 36 reduces to one out of six.

Many children are diagnosed with disorders of attention. Some children are said to have attention deficit disorder hyperactive type, some are said to have attention deficit disorder inattentive type. Some children are brutally misdiagnosed and just need to go out and play.

Hyper-Vigilant Attentive Disorder, on the other hand, is not a diagnosis. Maybe it should be.

Hyper-Vigilant Attentive Disorder

As I'm writing this book, I am also actively, if sporadically, engaged in returning phone calls, answering emails, planning my next trip to see therapeutic boarding schools in Utah, thinking about what I'm going to get for my wife for her birthday, and giving some serious thought to the clients I'm going to see later today. Oh, and there goes a squirrel outside the window. What a beautiful, big, bushy tail she has.

207

I'm glad I didn't miss seeing her.

Because if I were afflicted with Hyper-Vigilant Attentive Disorder, I might have been ultra-focused on this one piece of writing and not have seen the squirrel at all.

Engrossed only in writing this article, absorbed in this one task, I might not have noticed the squirrel. Ignoring the squirrel, I would not have reflected on how she might have been looking for nuts, which, in turn, would not have allowed me to remember how much I like salted cashews. Not flashing on salted cashews would have caused me to forget to consult my list for the market—bread, milk, eggs, raspberries if they're on sale—where I had jotted down a note about reading some essays that I had promised to some of my college admissions counseling kids. I'm just grateful that I don't suffer from Hyper-Vigilant Attentive Disorder because I could have missed it.

***

There's an Einstein story that goes something like this: Einstein spent decades trying to come up with a grand unified theory (GUT). Einstein would work on parts of the GUT problem at his home in Princeton. Wearing rumpled trousers, a sweater, and socks, he would cover blackboard after blackboard with arcane equations. And he would get stuck. Twelve or fourteen hours of the greatest pure-thought guy the world has ever seen thinking about a part of this GUT problem and he's S-T-U-C-K, throw-the-chalk-at-the-board, the-heck-with-it done.

So he'd do what any greatest intellect in the history of the world would do: have a snack and go to bed.

And in the morning, he'd pick up the chalk and write down the answer, the answer that had come to him in the night as he slept, the answer that had come to him while he was thinking about something else entirely.

In the six decades since Einstein's death, no one has made significant progress on this problem, the invention of high-speed computers notwithstanding.

The point being that—for want of a more articulate explanation—there are "people" living in your head. You don't know their names; you don't know

208

their addresses; you can't "call" on them when you want them, but they're there. Sometimes you can access these folks and the information they have and sometimes you can't. Don't believe me? Think that you're the one and only captain of your ship? Then why can you sometimes remember stuff and sometimes not?

Here's an even simpler explanation: How come you can usually find where you put your keys?
And sometimes not?

***

Which brings us back to the problem of what to do with those students among us who are afflicted with Hyper-Vigilant Attentive Disorder, those poor souls who can't think of more than one thing at a time. It has been suggested that we put them in "special" classrooms with a label on the door that says, "These poor thud-puckers think differently." Then we can "treat" them with "strategies."

***

Attentive readers will know how often I refer to the facts that women in this country were not allowed to vote until 1920 and that there were few women in college or university until just a generation ago. The number of women in my dad's law school class was three; now there are more women in college and more women in medical school than there are men. But for hundreds of years, women were excluded from higher education because they were thought to be unable. As Dr. Johnson said, "Sir, a woman's preaching is like a dog's walking on his hind legs. It is not done well; but you are surprised to find it done at all."

Similarly, aren't we "throwing away" those who learn differently? If you wouldn't shop in a shoe store with a "one size fits all" philosophy, why do you tolerate a community where many schools still treat all students as if they all learn the same?

I'd write more about this topic, but I'm off to the store to pick up a few things—salted cashews for example. I'm hoping that along the way, I'll figure out what to get my wife for her birthday!

58

Love your kids for who they are, not what they do; love your kids for who they are, not where they go to college.

The Best College

I'm going to go out on a limb here and suggest that Tom Brady is a significantly better quarterback than Tim Tebow.

In ten seasons, Brady has appeared in five Super Bowls, winning three of them. His career post-season record of 16-5 is unparalleled. Brady has won two Super Bowl Most Valuable Player Awards and has been invited to seven Pro Bowls.

Tim Tebow—his alliterative name notwithstanding—has done none of those things. Tebow has appeared in no Super Bowls (you would know if he had), has never been invited to start in a Pro Bowl, and does not have 16 post-season wins. As of this writing, it is unclear whether or not Tim Tebow is even a quarterback with an NFL team.

By any objective measure, Tom Brady is a better quarterback than Tim Tebow.

Unless, of course, we look a little more closely at the "objective measure."

Because if by better quarterback we mean the one with the most passing yards or the one with the most post-season wins, then the better quarterback is Tom Brady, by a mile and a half. But if better quarterback is defined as the one who can sell more tickets or who has a longer time horizon or who is the more eligible bachelor, then an argument can be made for Tim Tebow. It's possible that Tebow will be able play longer because he's younger, and is single. Brady is married and nearing retirement age.

The topic of an absolute "good" goes back to Plato's philosophical discourses of 2,500 years ago. Here are a couple phrases from Wikipedia on the subject: "Good is the ultimate object of knowledge," and "the Good makes all other universals intelligible." Simply stated, "Good is good."

Tom Stoppard suggested that the tune of a Mozart concerto is better than the sound of a trumpet being sawed in half or a parrot being pushed downstairs inside a file cabinet. And I agree. Buy it's harder to agree whether a Mozart concerto is "better" than a minuet by Beethoven.

It is also hard to define a good woman. Sophia Vergara has a lot of money, is a movie star, and is very pretty. Should I marry Sophia Vergara? Should I devote my life to courting her? Should I write her poetry and play guitar outsider her window? Should I give up on the possibility of happiness with any other woman? Or should only Sophia Vergara—wealthy, movie star, physically attractive—be my goal?

Ignoring for a moment that I am happily married (and that were I to stray, my wonderful wife would chop me up into little pieces and feed me to the dog), what if Sophia Vergara leaves her sweaty socks on the floor of the bathroom when she comes back from a jog? If I insist that my bathroom floor remain unencumbered by stinky footwear, then Sophia—her other attributes notwithstanding—is not the woman for me.

What is the best college? Clearly Harvard, many would argue. Because Harvard admits only 6% of its applicants; because Harvard grads go on to graduate and professional schools; because Harvard is located in Boston, a great college town.

But what if, because Harvard admits only one student from every 16 applicants, your application is not the one smiled upon? What if Harvard grads go on to graduate school because of who the students were going in, not because of anything they learned in Cambridge? And what if Boston— wonderful city that it is—is just too distracting for some students? What if some students thrive in more rural neighborhoods?

Not to take anything away from Harvard, but it isn't for everyone.

Whoever said "college is a match to be made, not a game to be won" got it right. Yet I see students year after year who "stalk" popular colleges the way an unhappy lover might commit himself to an unobtainable—and in many cases inappropriate—woman. My argument—find out where you belong—is not sour grapes. It's about finding the best possible grapes—grapes that don't leave their sweaty socks on the floor of your bathroom.

59

It's much easier to make predictions about how kids will turn out AFTER the results are known. Making guesses about who will end up in college and who will end up in prison beforehand is much more difficult.

What's the Difference?

Javier's and Alejandro's parents could have been in the same Lamaze class. Born days apart but in the same hospital in 1987, the children have followed almost identical courses: learning differences and attentional issues that turned into trouble in school lead to evaluations that turned up no psychopathology, just the high verbal IQ and low processing speed frequently associated with kids who have trouble getting their homework done. Both Javier's and Alejandro's middle-class parents hired wonderful, supportive, creative tutors not just to remediate or get the children "up to grade level," but to make the curriculum meaningful and get the children turned on to the joy of learning.

In short, their parents did everything right, but the children turned out horribly wrong.

Both Javi and Alex started smoking pot in the ninth grade; both were dealing by the end of sophomore year. Both boys became increasingly disrespectful at home, bordering on oppositional and defiant. Lies flowed like water in both homes:

"I didn't have any homework, and besides I already did it."
"I would have been home by curfew but there was an accident on the Interstate."
"The marijuana isn't mine. My friend must have put it in my backpack."

When Javi was expelled from school for repeatedly skipping class and refusing to comply with any rules, his parents approached me about how to get their son back on the right path. When Alex was arrested for burglary ("It wasn't my fault; we were just hanging out by the pool") his parents came to me for a recommendation about wilderness therapy.

I counseled the families about the appropriate programs, eight weeks in the woods followed by a year at a therapeutic boarding school. Both boys had to be escorted, or "gooned" as they called it—picked up at four in the morning by trained escorts and taken to the program.

Both boys made progress. Neither Javi nor Alex smoked pot or took Xanax for 12 months. Both boys learned how to compensate for their learning differences and made tremendous strides academically. Both boys came home clean and sober with good attitudes about education and optimism for their futures.

Fast-forward five years.

I spoke to both families recently. Javi has slipped back into his reliance on substances. Only now his drug of choice involves IV needles rather than rolling papers. He has been in and out of rehab four times. His parents have tried tough love, intensive out patient, twelve-step, active recovery, everything you can name. Javi has even been in jail for his addiction issues, but is still unable to stay clean for more than three months at a time.

In his parent's opinion, their son is a "dead man walking." His judgment is so impaired, his self-esteem so low, his future so limited that it is only a manner of time before he overdoses, commits another drug related crime and is shot by a police officer, or wanders into oncoming traffic. Of course his parents are devastated.

Meanwhile, Alex has just finished his Master's in Business Administration.

How is it possible that these two young men, practically identical in every respect of ethnicity, religion, geography, family background, cognitive profile, right down to their sub-scores on their IQ tests could have such markedly different life paths? And what do these outcomes say about our ability to predict who will end up in jail and who will end up in a boardroom?

In retrospect it is easy to point fingers, throw stones, and tell Javi's parents what they did wrong: you should have got him into treatment sooner, you should have known he was smoking pot in ninth grade, you should have taken him to a psychiatrist rather than to a psychologist, you should have bottle fed rather than nursed. You should have stood on your head.

As anyone who has ever watched a sporting event or made an investment will tell you, if you want to have an arrow in the exact middle of the target, it is easier to shoot the arrow, THEN paint the target. "I knew it!" we all exclaim.

After the event.

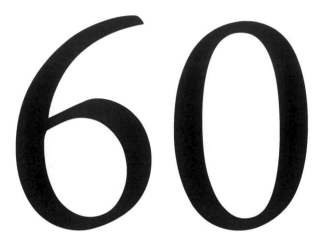

As always, the obsessions of narcissistic moms insisting that their children be number one leave me with a cold feeling. Would you want to trade lives with the speaker of the following? I wouldn't either.

Angel's Landing

Angel's Landing is the best hike in Zion National Park. It is the most arduous and the steepest. The hike to Angel's Landing takes the most time, climbs to the highest point, and has the best view at the top. In fact, Angel's Landing is so difficult that six people have died attempting to reach the top since 2002. For the last half-mile, there are chains to help keep hikers from being blown off the mountain. There is no room for error. One misstep, one inattentive moment and—pow!—3,000 feet down to dismemberment and death. It is important to hang on to the chains especially when the wind is blowing. From what I understand, the wind is always blowing.

No other hike in the park is nearly as difficult; therefore, no other hike is

216

nearly as good. One of the other hikes in Zion, Emerald Pools, does not have nearly as much vertical change. The path to Emerald Pools winds gently through a forest inhabited by deer and chipmunks. On occasion, hikers see foxes or colorful, non-venomous snakes. They say that the Emerald Pools hike gives time for both literal and metaphorical reflection.

Ha! I have no time or need for either.

I chose the hardest, most arduous hike and, although I was almost blown away by strong winds, hung on to the chain for dear life, and was terrorized for much of the seven-hour climb, I made it to the top. Of course, there was no time to look around—I had to get back down by nightfall—but that doesn't matter. Admittedly, I developed an eating disorder and a nervous tic on the way to the top, but who cares? A lifetime of misery is a small price to pay for achieving the summit. It's not the view that matters; it's getting to the top that is important.

Other lesser people went on different hikes. Their view wasn't as good even if they did waste time "enjoying the view." There is only one path to the top. Emerald Pools? Two words: "Pah" and "thetic"!

Of course, I want the same thing for my children.

Just the other day for example, my child came home from school where she takes three advanced placement classes as a tenth grader. She had been to her daily three-hour heptathlon practice after school. My daughter is the county champion at 800 meters, but her javelin throw is weak. I told her that I would not be proud of her until and unless she is the county champion in the javelin throw and all other events. After dinner, an activity that I limit to eight minutes so that she can be most productive, she went to her room to study. After three hours of studying, she fell asleep at her desk with the light on and a book in her lap. I shook her awake. I told her that she must study harder in order to get to the top.

We are surrounded in this country by those who are willing to settle for mediocrity. My child will get to the top. My daughter will go to a top school.

An eating disorder, a nervous tic, and constant fear of being blown off the mountain to her death are all small prices to pay for getting to the top.

The special times with our children are memorable and wonderful because they are rare.

Runable Moments

My regular gentle readers will know how committed—"obsessed" is such an ugly word—I am to running. I love my running buddies; I love the fact that my risk of dropping dead of heart disease is reduced as a result of our early morning workouts; I love the fact that every now and again someone says something so precious that the words resonate and are worthy of this very column.

Although the fact is that we get a true gem only every several thousand miles or so.* More on this ratio later.

Asking in advance for your patience and forgiveness—sign here; initial here and here—and in the spirit of "you had to be there," here are two of my favorite running stories:

1) My buddy Daniel—a professor, but otherwise a pleasant enough guy—was saying hello to pretty much everyone whom we trotted past on the track one early morning. "Pedro, how's the family?" "Nice to see you, Tim." "Vilma, you look strong."

I told him that he was so popular and personable that he should run for mayor. Focusing on his workout and without missing a step, Daniel furrowed his brow and replied, "How far is it?"

2) This next vignette does better in the first person: "Grete Waitz won the New York Marathon nine times and earned a silver medal in the 1984 Olympics in Los Angeles. She and I were within a hundred yards of one another for 45 minutes in the Miami Marathon.

Then the race started.**

Okay, that's pretty much all I've got after 30 years of running and enough miles to have circled the earth at the equator. Let's take the conversation back to parenting, an equally sweaty occupation, but unlike running, one about which you never get to say, "It feels so good to stop."

In order for there to be special moments, there have to be a lot of un-special moments. A boatload of un-special moments by my count. A truly huge number of un-special moments. Tons of 'em.

That happy family where the kids take out the trash without being asked? The one where the adolescents make dinner and say thank you to their parents for working so hard? The one where the kids read books and eschew violent video games?

Along with working shepherds and successful athletes who don't practice, I hear about such families more often than I meet with them. Remember the Walton Family? Sure you do. Because they were a TV show. The Ingalls from *Little House on the Prairie*? Also exaggerated. And about a previous and therefore easy to romanticize century. I suspect the reality was significantly less glamorous.

219

In real life, you get to have that occasional, touching, important conversation with your adolescent child BECAUSE the moment is so rare. If you have the "respect women" talk with your teenage son more than once a year, then by definition, you're nagging. (Recommendation: have the talk about reproductive biology in the car while you're driving 70 miles per hour on the Interstate. If you have the sex talk while you're only driving 40 miles per hour, you run the risk that your child will hurl himself out of the car window.)

What's the take away for parents trying to raise healthy kids in a culture seemingly designed to make our children entitled, addicted, snarky, and oppositional?

The teachable moments come occasionally. Likewise, during those six a.m. runs through Matheson Hammock Park, it's rare to see something extraordinary. Here's the scorecard:

Number of six a.m. runs during which we saw no animal bigger than a mosquito: 512
Number of six a.m. runs during which we saw two bottle-nosed dolphins cavorting only a few feet from shore: 1

Like Stephen Breyer says about getting appointed to the Supreme Court, "It's important to be on the corner when the bus goes by." The more time you spend with your kids just talking about nothing, the more open they will be to listen when you have something important to say.

And what could be more special than that?

* For the truly math-y, here's the arithmetic: twenty miles per week times 50 weeks per year times 30 years equals 30,000 miles. I remember about a dozen clever remarks of which the two above are—arguably—worth repeating.

** I ran pretty well that day. Grete beat me by barely over an hour.

62

The following story is true. The names haven't even been changed.

Why Do We Have an Issue with Kids and Drugs?

The other evening, my older son sliced open the side of his finger. We took a pleasant drive over to the Emergency Room at ten o'clock and by five the next morning, he was sewn up as good as new. The doctor was thoughtful and competent—it turned out our kids had gone to school together—and, as we were leaving, he handed me a prescription that I dutifully filled after dropping my son at home.

Ellery's request that I wake him up and take him to school in an hour notwithstanding, I let him sleep off the effects of the anesthesia. When he awoke at the crack of noon, I asked him how he was feeling. He acknowledged that his finger hurt pretty badly, that he was in fairly severe discomfort. Even though I had 20 Oxycodone in my pocket, I gave my son an

221

Advil. When he woke up again at four that afternoon, I asked him again how bad the pain was. "I can handle it," he said.

Then, having missed a couple meals while he was being sewn up and sleeping, my adolescent son sat down to eat a plate of fried vegetables only slightly larger than his head.

The point of this vignette is not to remind my gentle readers that I am psychotically anti-pain medication. Yes, I am concerned about the rising tide of prescription drug use, but were one of my loved ones suffering through chemotherapy, I would do whatever I needed to do to ensure that my family member would have access to, say, medical marijuana. No, I am only mildly impaired on the subject of pain meds.

Nor is the point of this story to argue that zero Oxycodone was the correct dosage. Another sensible father might have given his teenage son an Oxycodone upon arriving home at six in the morning and another pill when the boy woke up for the second time at four in the afternoon. Had Ellery been in worse pain, I would have given him a pill or two.

The point of this article is to express concern over the fact that where reasonable people could agree to disagree over whether zero or two Oxycodone was the correct number, NO LOVING PARENT IN HIS RIGHT MIND would give an adolescent a series of 20 powerful narcotics over the course of a week. My son had a bad boo-boo on his finger; he did not have a cannon ball tear off his leg at the hip.

Oxycodone is an opiate narcotic or analgesic—I'm copying from the website here—that "changes the way the brain and nervous system respond to pain." I like my son's brain just fine the way it is, thank you just the same. I am completely satisfied with the boy—his prodigious appetite for fried vegetables notwithstanding.

Wendell Phillips (not Thomas Jefferson as is commonly believed) said that "eternal vigilance is the price of liberty." Lao-tzu said, "The longest journey begins with a single step." I am not the first to remark that every drug addict was born clean. I am going to suggest that if you want your kids to grow up relying on themselves rather than on your medicine cabinet, yesterday would be a good time to start. Because you have to fight this fight every single day. Your kids will be offered drugs of some kind—at school, on TV, by the doctor, by a relative—each and every day. In 2013, DAILY vigilance is the price of a non-addicted child.

I am not advocating for pain. (The Pain Lobby gets few contributions, I feel certain.) I am not in favor of depression. (I am equally convinced that the Depression Political Action Committee has no members with whom I would wish to have a conversation.) Only a zealot would argue against narcotics, psycho-stimulants, and SSRIs for those who need truly them. I am suggesting that for a generation that doesn't remember life without the expression, "There's an AP for that," we have to be careful that they don't also believe "There's a pill for that."

No one wants to watch his child be in pain, depressed, or doing badly in school.

But no one wants to watch his child in treatment for addiction to prescription medications either.

In no other country are pain medications dispensed so freely. At no point in the history of civilization have pain medications been so easily available. It's time for the pendulum to swing back toward the World War II slogan, "Make it do or do without." Because I have to wonder how many of the 2.3 million folks in this country incarcerated for drug related offenses started out in the ER with their dads with a prescription for painkillers from a well-meaning doctor.

63

You can't pretend to know how someone else's mind works. Brains are just too complex. Therefore, it is in your interest and your children's interest to allow them to derive their own meaning and figure out how to learn on their own.

This Brain is Your Brain

There is a story about Enrico Fermi, the great 20th century physicist. A graduate student is trying to impress the professor by spewing off a litany of sub-atomic particles. Fermi puts the student in his place by responding, "Young man, if I could remember the names of those particles, I would have been a botanist."

Why do generations of physics students love this story? Is it the put down that resonates so soundly? "I am a pure thought guy," communicated the older scientist. "You cannot play in my league if all you can do is memorize."

224

Surely with technology, memorization of facts is less important now than in previous generations when access to information was sporadic. The capitals of the states, the books of the Bible, the name of the Vice Presidents chronologically or alphabetically—all are available with a few clicks. There's a third "zing" from the Fermi story that I like even better than the "put down" and the "thinking is better than memorizing" take-aways. I like the "all minds are different" punch line. Fermi won a Nobel Prize for physics in 1938; he worked on the Manhattan project helping to develop the atomic bomb; he has a class of sub-atomic particles named after him*. In short, he was one of the greatest physicists of the modern age.

But he would have been a lousy botanist.

We need physicists and we need botanists. We need memorizers and we need pure thinkers. Of course, no one would be so short-sighted as to argue that these categories are truly dichotomous. The best memorizers need to do some thinking and the best thinkers need to do some memorizing. There is room in our culture for all kinds of brains.

Is there room in your home for different learning styles?

Or when your kid comes home excited about learning Spanish, do you force her to do math? When your son comes home from school eager to finish reading *Sounder*, do you insist that he do math worksheets? When your daughter walks in the door excited about learning math, do you insist that she read a book instead? If your daughter wants to take apart a car engine, do you tell her to get back to her sewing?

Were Enrico Fermi your son, would you have discouraged him from studying physics?

So there is no possible misunderstanding, let me clarify that the following is okay: if your child comes home from school excited about playing "Shoot, Shoot, Shoot, Blood, Blood, Blood, Kill, Kill, Kill," that child should be redirected to reading a book or engaging in some other activity that will not put him solidly on the path to rehab for video game addiction. Also not okay: if your child comes home and says, "What I'm best at and what interests me the most is smoking pot so rather than helping to cook dinner, I'm going to drive around town and blow dope."

225

It is appropriate to allow our children to choose their own path; they will walk farther in the right direction if we do. By forcing—or attempting to force—kids to study what we want, how we want, and when we want, we lessen the likelihood that they will end up in the right place—on the dais in Stockholm or under the hood of a car.

* Fermions. Which include quarks and leptons. How cool is that?

64

Metaphors, as well as actions, communicate more effectively than words. In general, words are highly over rated.

I Never Metaphor I Didn't Like

Before touring a wilderness therapy program in Hawaii this past March, my wife and I arrived a day early so that we could enjoy the sights of the Big Island. One of our tourist stops was Volcano National Park. My wife, the science teacher, began talking about volcano bombs, magma, fault lines, and lava flow. As I heard her descriptions and saw the extent of the volcano, I was convinced that nothing could ever grow where the molten rock had flowed. Surely the devastation would be endless and forever. What could ever grow where there had been temperatures high enough to melt rocks?

Yet there were trees everywhere. Growing out of black rocks, out of the bleak and desolate landscape, were trees. My wife pointed out that after the volcano destroys everything in its path, new, rich soil is left behind out of which new growth springs forth. Young plants that would not have had a chance of survival in the plush forest can now thrive.

This growth out of rocky devastation reminds me of a self-destructive adolescent whose drug and alcohol use can be so out of control that the smart money would predict that nothing positive could ever come from him. A 16-year-old who usually refuses to go to school and does no work when he does show up, a young man who blames everything and everyone rather than looking inward—what hope is there? Is it possible to get past the anger and oppositionality? Can a productive, content life ever follow?

These young men have diets that consist of potato chips and ice cream rather than whole grains, bananas, carrots, and celery. Rather than conversations and meaningful interactions with other people, these young people play "Shoot, Shoot, Shoot, Blood, Blood, Blood, Kill, Kill, Kill" hour after tedious hour.

But from this unhealthy diet and stunted growth can come rebirth. Like the trees growing on the barren lava fields, it takes a little luck and a lot of hard work for roots to take hold. A significant change of landscape is required, frequently wilderness therapy followed by therapeutic boarding school, but transformative positive change in possible.

***

The take away? Even the most damaged kids have a shot at healthy, productive lives.

Oh, and one more point: all meaningful learning is metaphorical.

In the description above, the analogy of an unhealthy diet of salt and sugar not being as healthy as one of fruits and vegetables makes the point that connecting with actual people is healthier than suckling on a video game. The metaphor of a tree growing in rocky soil speaks to the defiant young man getting healthy in a new environment. Imagine these points without the metaphors. It's not about good writing; it's about adequate communication.

Not only do actions speak louder than words, words don't mean anything at all unless backed up by information our children can process. And our children seldom process words.

228

That's why we have to take our kids places—hiking and camping in the mountains if we can afford the time away from work and the cost of airfare or to the park at the edge of town if our time and finances are more limited. "I love you and would do anything for you" is a nice sentence. Sitting silently watching the sun go down over the mountains conveys the same information in a significantly more powerful and visceral way.

Consider the following communication: "You can do it; I have faith in you; I trust your judgment; I will never give up on you." But when the child tries to do anything, the parent is right there to make sure the task gets done properly—whether or not the child is involved. As has often been said, self-esteem doesn't come from never failing; self-esteem comes from overcoming failure. Sure, it's hard to watch your ten-year-old child try repeatedly to build a fire. But if you can watch her try and fail, try and fail, you will communicate to her that you believe she can persevere and succeed. By watching her fail, you let her know that she can succeed without you jumping in and doing the task for her.

And isn't that message—that you believe in her, that you know she can do it without your help—what you wanted her to know in the first place?

There is information about good parenting everywhere. We just have to know where to look and how to interpret it.

Eternal Vigilance

Forty-year-old Juan is a two-pack-a-day smoker with a sedentary lifestyle and a tire around his tummy that makes the Michelin man look *svelte* by comparison. Juan can, and frequently does, suck down a six-pack of Bud on a Sunday afternoon while watching his beloved Marlins. "Exercise" consists of walking from the couch to the fridge to get another cold one. "Camping" is defined as staying in a hotel room where the tiles in the bathroom don't go all the way to the ceiling.

Feeling a repeated tightening in his chest one day, Juan goes to a doctor whom he hasn't seen since they were in math class together in high school. The doctor is explicit: "Change your lifestyle," he begins. "Or die." Juan asks for a second opinion. "You're ugly too," the doctor deadpans. Just kidding.

The doctor says that in order for Juan to avoid an invasive, intrusive open-heart procedure, there is only one alternative. Juan must start exercising consistently and drop the 40 pounds. Otherwise, he'll have his chest cut open and spend several days with inconvenient tubes stuck in his body.

So the very next day, Juan goes out for a run. He was a three-sport athlete in high school after all—thirty years ago, admittedly—but he knows how this works. How hard can it be? When the alarm goes off at 6:00 am, he laces up his new $120 running shoes and hits the street. He jogs expectantly to the end of the block, a distance of some 200 yards, where he proceeds to do the following: he stops running; he bends over and holds his knees; he notices that he is sweating uncontrollably and that his heart is beating 160 times per minute; he looks around to make sure he's not being observed. Then he walks slowly back to his house exhausted, embarrassed, and dejected.

But the next day the alarm goes off again at 6:00. This time, Juan runs more slowly and is able to cover 300 yards—still only a three-minute workout—before walking home. But within a month of running six days a week, Juan runs a full mile. Exhilarated, he celebrates by not having any ice cream and quitting cigarettes. A year later, Juan enters a ten-kilometer (six-mile) race. He doesn't win, but he doesn't finish last either. "I went from not being able to run around the block to running six miles without stopping," he tells me. "Think I give a s**t about my time?"

Juan continues to run six days a week. He never misses a day. He runs through both of our seasons here in Miami—construction and hurricane. He runs when the temperature hits 90 degrees before he gets home at 8:00 am; he runs during thunderstorms; he runs when he feels like running; he runs when he feels like any other activity—an un-anaesthetized colonoscopy, for example—would be vastly preferable to going out for a run.

Over the course of 24 months, Juan loses the 40 pounds. He no longer smokes cigarettes, although he still has a beer or two while watching the Marlins on Sunday afternoon.

Two years to the day after his visit to the doctor—in what can only be described as a triumph of the human spirit—Juan signs up to run his first marathon.

***

Parenting is the same. It's not about making a plan; it's about living the plan. It's not about saying what you're going to do; it's about doing it.

Every day, all day, the forces of evil are trying to mess up our kids. Someone is trying to sell our kids cigarettes. Someone is trying to lure our children into a life of addiction. (And don't even tell me about how cigarette manufacturers make cigarettes only for those who choose to smoke. Without smokers, there are no cigarettes companies. Period. Cigarette manufacturers need smokers. Your children will do just fine, thank you.)

Eternal vigilance is the price of liberty*. In this generation, eternal vigilance is the price of bringing up kids who aren't addicted to that which will harm them.

When your kids ask you if they can play a video game—"just for a few minutes"—say no. "World of War-Crack" didn't get it's nick name randomly. When your kids say, "All the other kids get to play video games," say no. Optionally, you can point out that all the other kids may not brush their teeth before bed, but in your family you do.

Good parenting in this generation is tough. But nobody said it was going to be easy. There are unprecedented forces aligned to make addicts of our children, to do our children harm. Ask the Juan of two years ago—holding his trembling knees 200 yards from his house.

* Wendell Phillips (1811–84)

How do sensible parents provide the economic and emotional support our children need without giving in to our children's wants?

The Worst of Times?

As a rising seventh grader in the summer of 1967, I was invited to lunch at the home of my future? band teacher. Mr. Abrams lived walking distance from the junior high where he taught and where I would soon attend. The meal was served by his wife, the mother of their three children. She did not work outside the home. I remember the youngest of Mr. Abrams' three kids as being a few years ahead of me. He played trumpet.

Because pretty much everyone in my family is employed as a teacher, I feel confident that the following numbers are truthful if not factual: I think Mr. Abrams earned around $8,000 a year—he taught summer school too—and that the fair market value of his four bedroom, three bath home was some $20K. The ratio of the value of his home to his yearly income was 2 ½. I'm a counselor, not a mortgage broker, but it is my understanding that these numbers make good financial sense—that the Abrams family could go on vacation and save for retirement, that they could have a life.

Fast forward 45 years. Even with the downturn in the Miami housing market, the fair value of that Coral Gables home is over half a million dollars.

And a Dade County Public School teacher earns $40K.

Were Mr. Abrams teaching today, he could not afford to live in that house. Even if his wife worked outside the home. Even if all three of his kids worked and contributed their entire earnings to the family coffers. Mr. Abrams can no longer afford to drive by that house—never mind live there and make payments.

***

So where do teachers live in Miami in 2012?

In apartments. With roommates. Far from the expensive neighborhoods in which their schools are located.

Or with their parents.

Middle school teachers in 2013 certainly don't live walking distance from their schools in two-thousand square foot homes.

***

That same year, 1967, Harvard tuition was $1,760. The minimum wage was $1.30. A Harvard undergraduate could work a full time job over the summer and put in 23 hours a week for the rest of the year to cover her tuition. That's a lot of working hours for a full time student—current thinking is that 10-12 hours of work each week is plenty—but it could be done.

Today, Harvard tuition is $37,576 for the year (ignoring another $3K in health services and student services fees which are hardly optional). A student earning the minimum wage of $8.00/hour would have to work 93 hours per week—an untenable schedule for even the most motivated and sleep-deprived young person.

234

In short, college students in my day could finance their educations even at expensive private schools. For our children, the arithmetic no longer works. No matter how hard they work, no matter how motivated they are, the numbers just don't add up. If our kids are going to go to college, we, their parents, have to pay.

***

Parents have been told for generations, "When your child turns 18, it's time to kick him out. The only way he will learn independence is if he is forced to live on his own, make his own way, get his own apartment, learn the harsh economic realities of making a budget and living within it.
The arithmetic no longer supports this "independence" argument.

There are those who argue that the college age children of today are coddled, that their parents pay too much attention to the self-esteem of their kids and put no emphasis on "can do." There are those who snort derisively about giving a ribbon to the kid who finishes eighth in an eight-person race. "I pulled myself up by my own boot straps," these folks say. "The children of today should do the same."

The reality is that these economic times are different from those of a generation ago. For better or worse, children today need our economic support. A case can be made that they need our emotional support as well.

Maybe the "science" of parenting is still a long way from anywhere. Maybe we know what not to do, but we still have a significant journey before we know what works even with the easiest children.

No, Your Children Aren't Born with a Book

Toward the end of the Second World War, one of my dad's buddies got an infection. He had a high fever and was admitted to the infirmary. His arm swelled up to three times its normal size. There was no doubt but that this young serviceman would die.

Except that a new kind of medicine, antibiotics, were now available to solders in 1945. My dad's buddy received a series of penicillin shots. Within a couple of weeks, he was as good as new and back to active duty.

Medicine, which did not exist previously, is now standard care. Information and treatments that were not known are now readily available. Few people with access to adequate healthcare die of infections anymore. Modern medical science also has inoculations. There is no reason for anyone to succumb to measles, mumps, rubella, or a host of other childhood diseases that, until 100 years ago, routinely killed children.

Of course, there are childhood diseases for which complete and total cures do not yet exist.
I would argue that there is an analogy in here for the new science of parenting—not that we have all the answers, only that we have made some significant progress in the past several generations.
Just like the rusty nail that nearly killed my dad's buddy 67 years ago, the threats to our children today are obvious. Before you dismiss any of the following as the stuff of hyperbolic fiction, let me assure you that each of these stories is taken directly from families with whom I am currently working:

Mrs. A smokes pot with her 16-year old daughter. Her "reasoning," such as it is, involves the following phrase: "I know that she's going to smoke marijuana; I'd rather that she did it at home, with me, where she'll be safe."

In actuality, this young woman does not HAVE to smoke marijuana. She smokes marijuana, at home or elsewhere, because her mother allows her to. Indeed, in a very real sense, her mother insists that her daughter smoke pot.

Mr. B. insists that it's okay for his son not to do any chores around the house. His "explanation" is that it's just too much trouble to stay on top of making his son take out the trash and set the table.

Denying a child the opportunity to make age-appropriate contributions to the family is a mild form of child abuse.

If "don't smoke pot with your child" and "allow your child to help out around the house" seem like large targets, let me now make the main point of this essay:

The most egregious form of inadequate parenting that I see year in and year out involves not accepting our children for who they are. Which is not to say that we must embrace mediocrity, only that trying to force your scholar to be a carpenter or your carpenter to be a scholar never works.

Replicated research corroborates that having high expectations with lots of unconditional affection frequently leads to having content, accomplished children. Telling your child with a visual processing issue that he'll "never amount to anything if he doesn't read more" does not.

On a deeply personal note, an old buddy of mine—a good friend from my childhood neighborhood—committed suicide recently. I would not presume to suggest what demons allowed him to leave his wife and grown children; my analysis would be so lacking in insight as to be meaningless. I do remember, though, the unending pressure from his mom that he attend medical school.

I can't help but wonder if he wouldn't have been happier had he felt that his life and his choices were more under his control. Better a happy doctor than a happy mechanic? Okay. But better a happy mechanic than a dead doctor, surely.

***

I know there are more questions here than answers. Who am I to say that my friend would have been happier had he studied another discipline? Maybe his sadness was unrelated to his profession or to his upbringing. Maybe no one can truly know the inner workings, the "dark 3:00 a.m. of the soul" of another.

Maybe the science in which I am interested—parenting—needs another 67 years to catch up to the science of infectious diseases.

68

Lest any gentle reader suggest that I am against "standards," "rigor," and other current meaningless "buzzwords", here is an essay about when it is appropriate to stop listening to your child and just say no.

Kate and Edith

"You're sending me away to boarding school," intones ninth-grader Melissa. "I'll never speak to you again."

"But, Honey, you know the local schools here are terrible," Mom responds. "You yourself said that you're not learning anything, that your teachers are uncaring and borderline abusive, that your classmates can barely read. You're the one who came up with the idea of boarding school in the first place. It wasn't even our idea."

"I don't care; I don't want to go; I hate you."

"Melissa, please try to understand. Your father and I are making big sacrifices—both emotional and economic. You yourself said you wanted to go to boarding school."

"I just said I'd go so you'd stop badgering me about it. I don't want to go. And I'm not going."

"You most certainly are going, Young Lady. Now go to your room. And as a punishment, you are limited to only five hours of Facebook and texting tonight instead of your usual six."

***

What's wrong with this picture? Only everything. Indeed these parents might want to throw away the entire conversation, keeping only the frame.

As parents, we are unlikely to be able to have it both ways. Our kids can like us. Or we can, now and again, not give our kids everything they want. We cannot "have our Kate and Edith too."

When was the last time a five-year-old waiting to get her immunizations for kindergarten said, "Yes, Mumsy, I acknowledge that there may be a modicum of physical discomfort involved in the forthcoming procedure, but I accept the necessity of these shots so that I may lessen the likelihood of contracting communicable diseases including, but not limited to, cholera, diphtheria, measles, mumps, and rubella."

To the contrary, every child in the pediatrician's office is hollering, "Don't let some stranger hold me down and stick metal in my arm!"

As unpleasant as it is to insist that your child go through the pain of shots, it's more difficult still to watch them and care for them with a real, honest-to-goodness, life-threatening disease.

Which brings me to some gentle advice regarding fussing children. If you have made up your mind that your decision is unequivocally in a child's best interest—getting shots, say—then listen patiently as they explicate chapter and verse why you are wrong, allow them to voice their views, nod as they gripe.

And then: don't respond.

Don't engage; don't get into it. Don't repeat your point of view. At the risk of comparing your beloved 14-year-old child to a well-known barn yarn animal: do not wrestle with a pig in mud. You'll just get dirty and the pig enjoys it.

Most decisions can and should involve your kids. Kids learn how to make good choices by—eh—making choices. Which shirt do you want to wear? What do you want to eat? With whom do you want to play? Do you want to help me wash the dog or help me clean the yard?

As kids get older, they should even be allowed to make bad decisions. Indeed, self-esteem comes not from never failing but from learning that failure means another chance rather than the end of the world. I didn't study and I got a C. Stuff happens.

And maybe I better study next time.

Your kids don't have to like you when they're kids. They'll like you well enough when they're older. It's our job as parents to give our kids what they need. It is also our job as parents to ignore what our kids want.

Otherwise, we'd acquiesce to their requests for ice cream for breakfast and unlimited access to "Shoot, Shoot, Shoot, Blood, Blood, Blood, Kill, Kill, Kill."

Being afraid of "What if my kids don't like me?" is not the opposite of compliance. But when you signed up to be a parent you agreed to make the tough calls on occasion—which involves, now and again, an unhappy child.

I hope you enjoy reading this as much as I enjoyed writing it. And yes—I assure you—every word is true.

Stupid

Here's an expression that I hear frequently (you may have even said the following words today): "That's the stupidest thing I've ever heard." Yeah? Bring it. You think you've got Stupid? Compared to what's been going on with me this week, you haven't ever even met Stupid. Stupid doesn't know where you live.

Top this: some months ago, I glanced out my window and happened to observe a young man wearing short pants and a gray shirt getting into my car. Certain that I had proffered no such invitation to any person wearing a shirt of any color, I scampered outside and engaged the crew-cut gentleman in conversation.

242

"What do you think you're doing?" I began.

"Yeah, man, it's okay. I'm leaving. It's okay," he replied.

Feeling strongly that it—whatever it turned out to be—was anything but "okay," I allowed the conversation to deteriorate. Admittedly, harsh words were spoken. Feeling that a further exchange of views was unlikely to be productive, I summoned the authorities who promptly apprehended said young man breaking into another car, this one belonging to a neighbor living three blocks away.

A series of civic responsibilities followed—identifications, depositions, phone calls with a series of prosecutors (each of whom asked the same questions), trips to various governmental monoliths conveniently located in cities in vague proximity to the one in which I live and where Mr. Grotlee and I had engaged in our brief, unsatisfying conversation.

Still, following through seemed like the right thing to do, an opportunity to teach the children about the criminal justice system ("Daaad, we already know that!") and a chance to ensure that Mr. Grotlee was incarcerated. I had no illusions about recovering the $5 and three CDs with which Mr. Grotlee has absconded. (Note to younger reader: CDs were a plastic medium, popular in previous generations, on which music or other binary data could be... Oh, never mind.)

But, getting back to Stupid: I am making no inference as to Mr. Grotlee's mental capability or lack thereof. If his nineteen previous arrests for drug-related crimes are any indication, it is his addiction issues, not his SAT scores, that are of concern. My story involves the series of robo-calls subsequent to Mr. Grotlee's release from the custody of the state, the first of which came at 9:30 on a school night last week.

"Blah, blah, blah, Grotlee. Blather, blather, blather, Grotlee," the recording began. "Released, doesn't matter, who cares?" it continued. "Grotlee, Grotlee, Grotlee." But then the recording got interesting: "To let us know that you have received this message, enter your pin. Otherwise,"—I was listening intently now—"we will call back every two hours."

As the great philosopher Scooby Doo so aptly expressed, "Rut ro!" Because I am unequivocal: I did not get a pin number when I went to the state attorney's office; I did not get a pin number when I went downtown; I did not get a pin number on a box. I did not get a pin number with a fox. And now the recording is going to call me back every two hours.

Which, with a precision that only Truly Stupid can achieve, they summarily proceeded to do.

The next call duly arrived at 11:30 pm, as promised. The one after that at 1:30 in the morning. Having tried every pin number I had ever used—but never guessing the mystery pin I had secretly been assigned—I unplugged the phone and got a glorious four hours of sleep before getting up to go run with the loonies and fulfill my other responsibilities during a day in which Roman legions thoughtfully marched repeatedly through my brain.

Eventually, I was able to contact someone of my own species in the Florida State Department of Criminal Sometimes We Put You on Hold Just to See How Long You'll Wait and determined that, indeed, my pin number was the last four digits of my phone number times my wife's social security number divided by the number of times I had thought about putting a fork in my eye the night when the robo-calls kept coming in.

"Of course," I said thankfully. "I should have known."

What's the takeaway? Surely, "avoid civic responsibility to decrease the likelihood of over-zealous phone recording programmers invading your home" cannot be right. Nor is "somebody should have mentioned to Mr. Grotlee that being chemically dependent on drugs in a bad life plan," that particular horse being not only out of the barn, but well down the road. Indeed, it could be argued that said horse had died some years ago, its bones long since rotting in the sun.

No, in my psychotic ravings that early morning, before pulling the phone out of the wall, I reflected on how unlikely it was that anyone would remember their (alleged) pin number at two-hour intervals.

Similarly, many of the parents with whom I work remind their children every two hours to do their homework. Ignoring for the moment whether or not homework is developmentally appropriate for young children (it's not), what makes parents think that incessant reminders will be of benefit?

244

As always, my advice is simple: avoid obsessing about insipid homework. Instead, sit down and read a book with your child. Your child will learn more and, in a relaxed household, you will be more able to keep an eye out for Mr. Grotlee breaking into your car.

Accept your children for who they are. It's not just a good idea; it should be the law. They can't change what they didn't choose.

Here's an Idea

Do any of the following monologues sound even remotely plausible? Is there a syllable of truth in any of them? The speakers are men aged 70, 10, and 40, respectively.

1) "I know what I'll do. I'll wake up this morning and pretend that I can't hear. That way, my wife of 40 years will yell at me and treat me like I have cognitive impairments or am a deranged psychopath."

2) "I have a plan. I'll refuse to learn how to read. Sure, I'm in fourth grade and all my classmates can read pretty well. But what I'll do is choose to make the letters dance around the page so that I'm unable to focus or figure out the words. That way my parents will rant at me and I'll get to go see opticians,

specialists, and therapists rather than playing outside with my friends. My life will become an unrelenting nightmare of power and control issues with my folks. I'll be accused of being unmotivated, uncaring, oppositional, and possessed by demons. But at least I won't have to read books and enjoy a pleasant childhood."

3) "I woke up this morning with an idea: I decided that going forward I will be attracted to people of my own gender. That way, I can be a pariah to my family, at risk of contracting a deadly disease, and have to hide my life from my coworkers. Yes, I was smart enough to graduate in the top twenty percent of my law school class. Yes, I was clever enough to get a job as a prosecutor with the state attorney's office. Yes, I am trusted by the State of New York to try Murder One cases. But no, I wasn't smart enough to choose to be heterosexual."

For the record: nobody ever chose to be deaf; nobody ever chose to have a reading disability; nobody ever chose to be gay. You wouldn't make these choices. Neither would anybody else.

What a liberating joy it is to love your kids for who they are rather than what they do. I love you when you spill your milk; I love you when you succeed; I love you when you fail.

What if your child were developmentally delayed? Would you love her any less? What if your child dropped the fly ball and lost the big game? Which is more important to you—that he be a sports hero or that he know he is loved? To whom is it important that he catch that ball, you or him? And if the answer is "I want him to catch the ball so that HE'LL be happy," you better be right about your motivation.

What if your child, in spite of his best efforts, couldn't get an A or graduate at the top of his class. (Arithmetic point: by definition, only one child can be first.)

How much of what our children don't do is "won't" and how much is "can't"? In my experience, parents are frequently disappointed with their children for that which their kids can't do. "Can't" becomes "won't" and then "won't" takes on a life of its own.

Take your kids at their word. If they say that CAN'T do something, believe them.

And love 'em and accept 'em anyway.

Because you can't change what they didn't choose.

71

What are you feeding your children? All loving parents stay away from fatty, unhealthy fast food. Are we feeding our children's emotional lives in a similarly sensible way?

What's Your Story?

There's a story about Abraham Lincoln growing up dirt poor, wanting to study but not having enough money to buy candles which would allow him to read after the sun went down. Gas lamps were also out of the budget and Mr. Edison's electric lights were a generation away. So instead of waking up at six a.m. to chop firewood, milk cows, and plow fields, Lincoln would get up at five a.m. so he could read for an hour by morning light. It is my understanding that Lincoln did not enroll in an SAT preparation seminar.

In my family, we tell the story of my grandmother who, in 1910 at 14 years of age, went to work in New York City. Having completed a secretarial course, she typed envelopes—one thousand envelopes each and every day. Her salary? A dollar—of which two nickels went to "car fare" (modern translation: "subway"), one nickel paid for lunch, and another nickel bought a soda pop. What did she do with the "net" profit—some 70 or 80 cents? See if you can determine what became of the funds from the following distinguishable choices:

a) She spent the profits however she darn well pleased. She earned it; the money was hers. She probably bought some "Hello Kitty" merchandise (she was, remember, all of 14 years old) or some frozen yogurt.

b) She bought a video game and some pot.

c) She returned home, cheerfully gave the money to her mother and thanked her mother for allowing her to go out of the house into the city to work. The alternative—carrying water for cooking and cleaning up five flights of stairs, making baby food from scratch for her seven younger siblings, and washing diapers (both electric washing machines and disposable nappies were generations in the future)—was less preferable. Work was a privilege.

My grandmother, after whom my oldest child is named, continued working as a secretary for the next seven decades. She even worked for FDR when he was assistant secretary of the navy. (Okay, so did dozens of other young women and my grandmother and FDR may not have spoken more than a few syllables to one another, but still: FDR!) She worked well into her 80s even after she tried to quit. Repeatedly. Her boss at the mortgage company, whom she had known for half a century, wouldn't let her retire. "You're the only one who knows where everything is," he would say. "Just come in for one more day."

This scenario—"C'mon; just come in and work for one more day"—went on for some years.

I like to think that had my grandmother been born in 1986 rather than 1896, that she might have been a college professor rather than a secretary. Her grammar, mechanics, and usage were perfect. She could proofread like nobody's business. You could throw a legal document across the room and before it hit the floor, my grandmother could tell you that there was a semicolon missing on page three. But there was no money for school—not for girls anyway—so she got along with what she had. Interestingly enough,

250

all four of her children have graduate degrees and all four of them have taught college.

Even though she's been gone 20 years, my grandmother is still a frequent topic of conversation in my family.

***

What are the stories that are the fabric of your family's life? Do you talk about the lives of great men like Lincoln and good women like my grandmother? Do you emphasize for your kids stories of resilience and sacrifice, of people overcoming hardship and making a life for themselves and their families? Do you feed your kids the "meat and potatoes" so that they know who they are, where they come from, and whom you admire?

Or do you feed your children potato chips and ice cream instead? Are the "heroes" at your dinner table those folks who have made a quick buck or been successful at the expense of someone else? Do you communicate to your children that you admire "winners" who use steroids and business people who have committed fraud to make their fortunes?

Are the sentences that narrate the stories of our families woven together from the strong thread of tales about good people doing the best they can? If not, tonight might be a good time to have your kids put down their video games and put down their homework worksheets so they can hear about the adversity that their great-grandparents overcame so that your kids can have a fridge full of food and a roof over their heads. Go ahead—turn on an electric light. There's no reason to wake up at five in the morning to tell your kids these stories about these good people.

And next time you think about giving in to your child's wants rather than focusing only on your child's needs, think about whether Lincoln and my grandmother worked hard and succeeded in spite of or BECAUSE OF the hardships they faced.

If your kids are listening, is it possible that you're talking too much rather than too little?

Listen. Do Wah Do. Do You Want to Know a Secret?

Why don't your children listen? Here's one possible answer: maybe your kids are bad. Why not? It's possible. Maybe deep down, they are just plain and simple, intrinsically B-A-D, bad, budding little rotten-to-the-core psychopaths who, left to their own devices, would deliberately, with malice of forethought, just refuse to listen because—stop me if I've mentioned this earlier in the paragraph—they are bad.

Maybe, to begin with Mom, you should admit to your husband that you also dated a space alien with a red cape and a pointy tail nine months before your B-A-D son was born.

Okay, I'm kidding. Not about who you may or may not have dated or what color cape he wore, but about the suggestion that your kids were born bad and are not listening because they are bad.

Your kids aren't bad.

So if they're not just bad, why don't they listen?

Here's a thought—and this one is serious: maybe your kids don't listen because you, their parents, keep telling them how to do every single, solitary little thing, no matter how minuscule, inconsequential, or unimportant. Maybe your kids are over it. The incessant, unceasing barrage of controlling words has forced them to build barriers to being receptive. Punch me in the nose often enough and I'm going to start putting my hands in front of my face.

How would you like a boss who told you how to do every aspect of your job? How would you respond to a spouse who insisted that you be physically intimate every Tuesday and Thursday at 10:05 pm? Wouldn't you agree that part of the joy of being alive is the ability to make choices, to determine your destiny, to finish your own sentences?

Your children would model how you live—if you would just hush up long enough for them to observe what your values are without being constantly harangued. All you're doing by talking all the time is modeling anxiety. If you could relax, they could listen.

How are they going to be able to tell the difference between that which is life-threatening—"Don't take drugs"—and that which is trivial—"Do this worksheet for homework"? If your anxiety won't allow you to tell the difference between critical and vacuous, how do you expect your children to be able to make that distinction?

No one would blame you for being anxious. Your community is a mess in ways that are new and worse, unprecedented really. Never before has a child had the opportunity to make such senseless, destructive decisions without guidance. Your children have access to that which is addictive and harmful in ways that previous generations did not. And they don't have to go any farther than the neighborhood convenience store to start down the path to poor choices and poor health. Twinkies, lottery tickets, alcohol and—if you live in

Colorado or California—marijuana, are readily available. Obesity, issues with gambling, alcohol and substance abuse are just down the street.

For Internet pornography, your children don't even have to go all the way to the corner. Any computer in your home will take your 15-year-old to photographs and videos that would make you cringe. You know the expressions, "You can't imagine?" In this case you don't want to.

What's the answer for parents? How about a little good old-fashioned silence? Combat the big things of which you disapprove by being quiet about the smaller things. Wait for the question.

"But if I don't tell him twenty times to get up and get dressed for school then he won't get up on time and he'll flunk his arithmetic test and he'll fail the fifth grade and he won't go to a good college and he'll grow up to drink wine in the gutter."

I wouldn't counsel against waking up an 11-year-old and telling him it's time to go to school. But I do wonder why the child isn't taking responsibility for setting his own alarm by that age. And if Mom actually is going back to wake him up repeatedly, don't you wonder if a change is called for?

So how do we get out kids to listen? How do we get them to comply? How do we get them to do what we know is in their long-term best interest? The seemingly contradictory answer is that if compliance is what you're after, the best you can hope to achieve is compliance. If you go to bars to meet partners, in all likelihood the partners you'll meet will be partners who go to bars. Not that there's anything wrong with bars, just that if you want to catch a trout, going fishing in a herring barrel in contraindicated.

The best parents I've seen over the years are the one who are content to just BE with their kids. (Pun intended.) Parents who wait for kids to ask a question before giving an answer do pretty well too. Or as a politician said in another context: "It's the relationship, stupid."

Take your kids hiking; let them choose a book and sit and read with them; take a walk with no destination, no agenda, and no time limit; turn off all the electronics and just sit in silence. Go toss a ball back and forth without speaking.

254

Yogi Berra taught us that "baseball is a fascinating game; you can see a lot of things just by watching." I would suggest that your children are indeed anything but B-A-D and that you can hear a lot of things—just by listening.

73

Allowing your children to make a contribution to the health of the household is a good way to bring up healthy children. I like to think that Thorton Wilder, author of "Our Town," would agree.

Translation

Pretty much everybody needs a little help deconstructing texts. It could be argued that the whole point of college is to learn how to read and understand Chaucer, Milton, Pope, and Shakespeare. Of course non-English majors learn how to understand different authors and ideas—Machiavelli for economics majors, Watson and Crick for biochemistry students.

"O, that this too too solid flesh would melt
Thaw and resolve itself into a dew!
Or that the Everlasting had not fix'd
His canon 'gainst self-slaughter"

My favorite professor at the University of Wisconsin, Richard Knowles, spent a semester helping me to understand—among others—these lines from *Hamlet*. Our boy is depressed but won't commit suicide because he believes that God forbids it.

Professor Knowles spent the better part of dozens of lectures teaching us how to translate early 17th century language and culture into words, ideas, and references we could understand and accept. What a decent, hardworking, wonderful professor he was. What a great course—a full semester of reading and talking about the plays of Shakespeare.

A generation later, one of the most successful college students I know is taking a course called "Epistomology and Phenomonogy." (No, I don't know what either of those words means either.) She reads the primary sources—Kierkegaard, among others, listens to lectures, and reads Spark Notes to make sure she understands the difference between "noesis" (real content) and "noema" (ideal content). (And no, I don't actually understand those words either. How many times do I have to tell you?)

In keeping with this proud tradition of translating text into terms that can be understood in modern times, here's one of my favorite passages from Thorton Wilder's 1938 "Our Town," an "allegorical representation of all life" according to one critic.

I'll parse out the paragraph in a minute but won't deny my gracious readers full access to one of the most moving dialogues of 20th century drama. The only context you need is that Dr. Gibbs is speaking to his 16-year-old son. The time of the play is just over a hundred years ago:

"Well, George, while I was in my office today I heard a funny sound ... and what do you think it was? It was your mother chopping wood. There you see your mother—getting up early; cooking meals all day long; washing and ironing;—and still she has to go out in the back yard and chop wood. I suppose she just got tired of asking you. She just gave up and decided it was easier to do it herself... Well, I knew all I had to do was call your attention to it. Here's a handkerchief, son."

Now here are the explications, the translations if you will, to a culture a century after the time about which Thorton Wilder was referencing.

257

"Well, George"

These two words refer to a time in which parents spoke to their children in respectful tones on a daily basis. Dr. Gibbs is addressing his son in a familiar way.

"...chopping wood..."

references a time in the history of our country when children were expected to do chores and make a contribution to the well-being of the household.

"Here's a handkerchief, son"

alludes to a time when children were exposed to guilt and shame is small, appropriate, healthy doses. Their behavior as well as their sense of self improved as a result. George is crying; but he'll get over it.

Without sarcasm or irony, here are the points of my gentle diatribe:

1) We no longer live in the safe, protected world of Grover's Corners where the biggest family issues were whether a junior in high school would play baseball with his friends before fulfilling his commitments to his family.

2) Although our 16-year-old children are under siege, attacked by sugary soft drinks and vodka, blindsided by tobacco and marijuana, it is still possible to bring up healthy kids.

3) "No" is still a powerful concept in raising healthy kids. The translation of "Give me a hand with chopping this wood" is simple: there's no better way to say "I love you" than to allow your children to help the family, to feel good about making a contribution, to be part of something bigger than themselves.

Loving parents spend too much time trying to ensure that their children know a little bit about too many subjects. They can do more harm than good.

Making a Difference

Here's a controversial sentence I bet you didn't think you'd read in a book written by a person who studied developmental psychology in graduate school, has dedicated his life to education, and makes his living giving advice to parents about how to bring up healthy kids. Here it goes:

For many neurotypical kids, it doesn't make a whole lot of difference what you do as parents.

For kids who "get it," for kids who learn quickly and efficiently, for kids who have both the horses (ability) and the whip (motivation), it doesn't make all that much difference what the teachers do. (I'm ignoring worksheets and other forms of abuse here.) It doesn't make that much difference what the

259

parents do. (Again, I'm ignoring abusive suggestions including "Put down that book, it's time to play video games and smoke pot.") Kids who CAN do pretty well, as long as we don't actively discourage them. Not that genes are destiny, but can you even give me that NAME of one of John Havilcek's coaches or Albert Einstein's teachers?

I didn't think so.

I could have coached John Havilcek—and I don't know a pick and roll from a Kaiser roll. I could have taught Einstein—and I don't know a muon from a moo cow. "Go play," I would have told both Havilcek and Einstein, and they would have achieved in spite of, not because of, my ability and insight as a coach or teacher. For talented athletes and super-able students, practice may make perfect, but the process is easier if you have a silk purse rather than a pig's ear to begin with. (It is said, by the way, that Einstein's teachers were anything but encouraging. Did he succeed because of or in spite of their advice?)

Parents claim credit for their high achieving kids. It's painful to me to hear this tripe. At the risk of being accused of sounding negative and critical— Moi?—I have to point out the absurdity of the following claim:

"MY daughter has 99th percentile test scores," says Mom at a party. This sentence is inevitably followed by a conspiratorial wink as if a stock tip about an IPO were forthcoming. "We READ to her when she was a child." The implication—that the parents of all those other children didn't think to pick up a copy of *Fox and Socks* is too offensive to refute. You read to your child? Good for you. Here's a cookie.

The issue here is "can't" versus "won't". A child who CAN put down her math book in order to pick up her reading assignments may certainly be encouraged so that she is exposed to proper doses of both magisteria. I revel in how much fun it is to teach those able children; I love inspiring their curiosity, engaging their ability to make inferences, connect disparate topics, pull together across disciplines. Who wouldn't want to teach such kids?

But those kids who excel across the board and who can change from one discipline to another don't need me all that much. Left in a sparsely furnished room with an organic chemistry book and a loaf of stale bread, they emerge with chapters memorized ready to take on the world.

260

I am much more interested in the child who CAN'T learn. Not to be confused with the kid who WON'T engage in and take responsibility for his learning. A child who, despite our best efforts, continues to have trouble with math SHOULD BE ALLOWED TO MOVE ON TO SOMETHING ELSE. Quite frankly, if I were locked in a room and told that I could come out when I learned to speak conversational French, well, let's just say that my heirs and assigns would be pretty pleased, because I would drop dead of starvation and fatigue before I got past "la plume de ma tante." I'm a nice guy. But I have no head for language acquisition.

Those of you who have never failed at anything, those of you who succeed where ever and whenever you put your mind to something, what do you think about the rest of us? Do you think we WANT to get lost? Do you think we're CHOOSING to have trouble in school? Do you think we're PLEASED about not being able to remember what seven times nine is? Do you think we're HAPPY about being held back, laughed at, and derided by our teachers, classmates, and parents?

We're acting out BECAUSE OF our learning differences. If we could learn the way you do, we would. Believe us. We see your awards for Student of the Month. We know how much better your lives are. We hear you when you say that you only had to study for an hour and you got an A anyway. We studied for three hours and got a lousy C. Again.

In the meantime, please let us learn something. Let us achieve where we can. Let us do a little more math and a little less language. Or the reverse. Comparing us to neurotypical kids helps no one. It makes us feel like we CHOSE to have the brains we have. You remind us of the teacher who said, "If you don't eat your meat, you can't have any pudding. How can you have any pudding if you don't eat your meat?"

For those of us who don't learn everything easily, it DOES matter what our teachers do. We need to be allowed to learn how we learn best. And if we're stuck on one subject, please do allow us to learn something else.

Otherwise, just go back to helping those kids who don't need your help, pretending that what you do for them makes all the difference.

75

Many adults can drink alcohol and not be alcoholics. Many children can play video games and not become addicted. Many children, but not all children. We are only beginning to appreciate the depths of the dependency felt by those who cannot easily put down their game console.

Video Killed the Radio Star

I've never asked Dennis and Joanie for money. But I could if I had to. If I couldn't make a mortgage payment, I'd ask them for a couple thousand to tide me over and they'd say, "You're sure you don't need more?" That's how close we are. That's the kind of people they are.

So while Joanie was griping at me this morning about how I just don't "get it" when it comes to video games and what a zealot I am and how I'm living in the dark ages and do I want to go back to prohibition, I realized that I must not have expressed myself well in our previous conversations and in this forum. Joanie is my good friend: I know she respects my opinions. If she doesn't understand my position, it's me. Clearly, I need to be more clear. (Obviously, I need to be more obvious?)

I have no problem with Joanie's argument: all video games are fun; good video games can teach empathy; great video games can be interactive in ways that books cannot. A truly great video game can bring spectrum-y kids together to work toward a common goal, allow Asberger-y children to connect with peers in ways they aren't able to do face to face. An extraordinary video game can teach lessons about economics, collaboration, even world peace. And these lessons can be visceral enough to "stick," to stay with kids long after a school curriculum has faded. "Besides," Joanie said triumphantly, "when was the last time you saw a kid spend 19 consecutive hours reading a text book?"

She went on: "There were times in this country's history when learning and performing music was frowned upon as a waste of time. There are religious zealots who discourage adherents from reading any book beside the Bible. There are crazy families who don't let their kids watch television." I nodded. "Good video games are no worse, as time wasters go, than reading novels, playing a musical instrument, or watching a ball game on TV."

Joanie went on to ask if I were a Luddite, against technology, in favor of forcing families to make their own furniture. Before I could say, "Have you BEEN to IKEA lately?" she went on to ask if I wanted to deny her a glass of Merlot on the weekends.

Feeling confident that it was my turn to talk, I assured Joanie that I wasn't going to come to her house with the Revenooers looking for moonshine and that, indeed, the next time my wife was over for dinner, I felt strongly that they should open a bottle of red as they have for years. I assuaged her concern that I want to forbid neurotypical kids from ever taking a study break to do some great brain teasers online or from relaxing with a RPG FPS.*

I have no issue with healthy kids relaxing with a video game. As long as they fulfill their other responsibilities to living a healthy life, as long as they put in a cameo at school, get some exercise, eat an occasional meal with the family, they can play "Shoot, Shoot, Shoot, Blood, Blood, Blood, Kill, Kill, Kill" to their heart's content. Similarly, Joanie can have a glass of wine and I can buy a lottery ticket. Who am I to say how you should live your contented life? I'm

263

even willing to try to understand how people who have never run a marathon can manage to say they are fully alive. (As it happens, Joanie has run several.)

My concern is with kids who play video games and are desperately unhappy as a result. I'm worried about kids who have an addiction they cannot control, who don't interact with other humans, who are angry and aggressive when they're not allowed to play their games.

I worry about kids who live in their basements, emerging only to eat unhealthy foods, whose virtual lives have become so much preferable to their real lives that their real lives are miserable.

Let's ignore the young man who starved to death after playing 50 consecutive hours of video games—true story. Let's allow that the couple who let their three-month-old baby starve to death while they were in an Internet cafe playing video games probably had other issues. Let's agree that for many kids under many circumstances, video games can be a pleasant addition to real life. But for many of the kids with whom I work, video gaming can be a deadly distraction. A lovely family I know negotiated with their son, a high school senior, to limit his gaming to 22 hours a week. Is it any surprise that the young man has trouble making friends or interacting successfully in the real world?

What's the take away for loving parents who want to help their kids grow up healthy and productive? A glass of wine a day is okay, a bottle of wine before breakfast is probably indicative of an issue with alcohol. Playing sporadic video games with other actual humans is preferable to holing up in a bunker for days at a time.

Maybe an even simpler explanation will serve: some can; some can't. Which kind of child do you have? A neurotypical, well-adjusted, focused kid who is going to be successful or a kid who is prone to addition and for whom video gaming will be an unrelenting nightmare? Have you made your choice? Are you sure your kid is the former, healthy one?

Would you bet your life on your insight? Would you bet your child's life?

* For those of you living next to me in this pleasant cave, RPG = "Role Playing Game" and FPS = "First Person Shooter."

264

76

Learning can be fun. Learning should be fun. As loving parents, we owe it to our children to help them find the best (read: hardest and most dedicated) teachers out there.

Three Times Seven

Bob Blitzer wasn't just a great math teacher; he was a good man. My first openly gay professor—and this was the early 70s—he was a force of nature in the classroom. He drew an inverted parabola on the board. "'Y equals negative X squared' looks like a missile," he began. "No, it doesn't. 'Y equals negative X squared' looks like a breast."

Can YOU think of a better way to engage adolescents in the subtleties of curve sketching?

Bob was a tireless advocate for struggling students. His office hours weren't Monday, Wednesday, Friday from 10:00 to 11:00 a.m. His office hours were any time he was awake. He taught like a mad dog. As long as you were willing to learn, he was willing to teach. No problem was too simple. From what I could tell, no problem was too complex either.

Most importantly, he could tell if you got it or not. If you got it, Bob would take you to the next concept in the sequence. If not, he would teach you the old concept in a new way. Until you did get it. If he ever got frustrated, I never picked up on it.

I may have forgotten some of the curriculum from that second semester calculus course 40 years ago. (Okay, let's face it: I may have forgotten ALL of the material from that second semester calculus course 40 years ago.) But I remember one pedagogical technique clearly. Bob and I were deep in some problem—finding the volume of a curvy three-dimensional object, say— when we came across some simple arithmetic. Bob paused in his explanation. "So, let's see, three times seven would be..."

His voice trailed off. I had been piping up, answering questions right along as Bob carried me through the intricate steps of the page long problem. But this time I stopped. "You know what three times seven is as well as I do," I said respectfully.

What Bob said next has stayed with me for four decades and through the thousands of students to whom I have taught math. "Yes. I just want to make sure you are comfortable as well."

Comfortable! In a math class. What a concept! Comfortable in an advanced math class no less, one with high expectations. (Bob's tests were brutal—no quarter asked or given. But if you had done every problem in the book three or four times and had studied until you starved to death, you could perform pretty well.)

Bob went on: "If you answer after I pause, then I know you've got it. You feel good and we go on to the next step. But if you don't speak up, you don't feel threatened." He paused as if deep in thought. "Math can be intimidating."

Imagine! Math as comfortable and non-threatening. In high school, my teachers had used their knowledge as a bludgeon. "I know this and you don't" had been their agenda. "And the reason that you don't know this is because you are fundamentally flawed." The antithesis of this attitude, the fact that

266

Bob and I were on the same team, that we both wanted the same thing, was empowering.

That's a great way to teach," I said.

Always modest about his ability, Bob replied, "Yeah, well, thanks. But I didn't think of it myself. I got it from this guy named Socrates."

***

How many of your children's teachers are communicating, "We're all in this together"? How often do your children come home saying, "We're learning this cool stuff; my teacher is really into it"?

On the other hand, how often do your children come home with worksheets assigned by teachers who are only concerned with quantifying that Tommy got 75 percent correct?

I'm not suggesting that as parents we must find the Bob Blitzers of the world. They are of a rare and possibly vanishing breed in an educational culture that values constant testing over shared engagement. I am hoping that you can allow your homes to be places where learning for its own sake has a place, where learning can be a hoot, where "Y equals negative X squared" can be a breast.

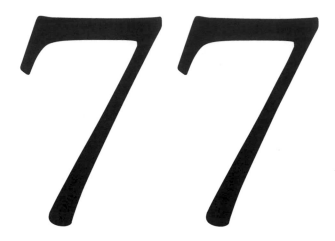

*Do you know everything that is in your own head? Do you know about your
learning style? If not, how can you be sure you are helping your child learn by
assuming you know how she learns and what is in her head?*

Chances Are

Consider all the money spent in the entertainment industry. Movies make up
the vast percentage of expenditures; books are almost an afterthought. Of all
the books that actually do get published each year, most are non-fiction—
calendars, cooks books, political biographies. Fiction is a tiny part of a
publisher's list. NEW fiction books have to compete with perennial best
sellers like *The Hobbit* and *Tom Sawyer.* Hence new fiction is a small part
of fiction. Poetry is the smallest percentage of fiction and poetry by new
authors is the smallest percentage of poetry. In short, the odds against a new
author getting a book of poetry published are enormous. You're more likely
to get bitten by a shark WHILE cashing your winning lottery ticket.

If all the books that have been published were lined up on one shelf and you picked one book at random, the chance that you would pick a book of new poems is effectively zero.

***

Imagine a list of the names of all the people alive today—a phone book, if you will, with seven billion entries. What is the likelihood that you would pick a name at random and want to have a conversation with that person? Even limiting the list to the people with whom you COULD have a conversation—not everybody speaks the language(s) that you do—chances are that you'd pick someone you didn't want to talk to. Even in this country, you could end up thinking, "You voted for THAT GUY? How could you vote for THAT GUY?" and wish you were speaking to someone else.

What about the odds of finding a song you'd like to listen to? Of all the genres of music and all the songs within those broad groupings, you could very well get rap if you like classical. Or the reverse. With millions of recording, if you're waiting for Bruce Springsteen's "Pink Cadillac" to come around on the dial, you'll have a long wait.

***

Most importantly, the odds of getting into someone else's head are the least likely of all. Because there are more people with more different learning styles than there are songs or books. Even the best teachers know the frustration. "How can she not understand that? I've explained it three different ways! How could ANYBODY not understand that?" But the fact is that she still just doesn't get it.

"Then she's not trying hard enough. She's lazy; she's unmotivated."

Maybe.

Or maybe she's not ready; maybe the curriculum isn't developmentally appropriate. Maybe she has learning differences; maybe she's got emotional issues that prevent her from attending to what you're saying and how you're saying it.

Maybe you just don't know what's in her head.

Because just like you have a tough time understanding how someone could vote for THAT GUY, or how someone could like THAT KIND of music, it's hard to know what's going on in someone else's head, what someone else's learning style is.

As teachers and parents, we have a choice. We can keep hammering away believing that we are right: everyone must learn THIS WAY. (Similar arguments: all Catholics should become Protestants; all atheists should become believers; all Republicrats should become Democans.)

Or we can embrace those whose learning styles are different from ours and invite a whole bunch more people to the party.

What do you think the chances are?

78

A 17-year-old child should be able to go to bed and wake up on her own. If not, something is wrong.

No Hats on the Bed

"No hats on the bed!" a woman screams at a visitor. "Get that hat off the bed! Now!"

"Okay," says the man. "But, by the way, why? Why must I take my hat off the bed?"

"Hats on the bed are bad luck! Terrible bad luck! Years and years of bad luck! Get that hat off the bed!"

"Okay," says the man. And he walks out of our scenario to appear in another chapter in some other book.

"My mother taught me that hats on the bed are bad luck just as her mother taught her. Everyone knows that hats on the bed are bad luck!" the woman shouts at the retreating figure.

Ignoring for a moment the silliness of all superstitions in general, why this particularly silly superstition—no hats on the bed—in particular? Some religious traditions such as not eating pork are said to originate from an evolutionary-adaptive imperative—trichinosis is said to be unpleasant. Could there be a REASON why this woman is hysterical about a hat on the bed?

I have been unable to trace this "no hats of the bed" belief to any specific country or culture. And I want my gentle readers to know that I googled "Hats on the Bed" and spent over two full minutes doing what can only be described as "Internet research."

Why did this woman's parents communicate so emphatically that hats on the bed are bad luck? Why will this woman tell to her children that hats on the bed are bad luck? Because in previous generations, hats on the bed spread head lice; there was good reason to forbid hats on the bed.

Today, with fewer hats and fewer head lice, this superstition could probably be put to rest. But what about the ANXIETY that goes with it? Clearly, in our evolutionary-adaptive environment, it was in our ancestors best interest to feel and express concern for their progeny. Anxiety was a good thing. If Percy T. Australopithecus was allowed to "go play in traffic" and got trampled by galumphing wildebeest, he was less likely to produce grandchildren than was Stacey who had to stay close to the home fires listening to why Grandma was having trouble with her email.

The other evolutionary-adaptive strategy, of course, was to give your kids calories in addition to information. As unfortunate as it is, no one ever got a chance to say, "Okay, I'll have the mastodon burger and fries and gimme a couple McArchaeopteryx combos for the kids." (C'mon, admit it. Don't YOU wish you could have had the chance to say that?) If you already had kids, then the imperative was to feed them so that they would have kids. Feed the kids first makes sense. That way, the kids survive and your genes get passed down. Let the kids have those yummy fat-rich mastodon burgers.

Fast forward a passel of generations and we have a problem: kids in my office have too many calories and too much anxiety.

272

There used to not be enough food. A great gift to children was extra calories. Now, the nicest thing we can do for our kids is to discourage them from absorbing every fat and sugar calorie in sight. Thirty percent of Americans are overweight with concomitant health concerns—higher risk for heart attack, stroke, and diabetes.

Kids are getting too many calories and kids are getting too much anxiety, neither of which is helpful any longer. It's time to cut back on the extra calories and rein in the anxiety.

"But if he doesn't study more, he won't go to a good college, and he'll end up living at home in the basement forever before going on to drink wine in the gutter."

Maybe.

But if your anxiety hasn't allowed him to make any decisions for himself since the day he was born, if you haven't allowed him to learn from failure, if you haven't given him the gift of figuring things out on his own, then why would he be able to make good decisions now that he's a teenager? You haven't communicated how to make sensible choices. To the contrary, you've communicated that the world is an unsafe place and that, without you poking him in the side so he can stay awake, he will fail and that the Earth (one of my favorite planets) will stop spinning. (Seriously, I work with parents who feel obligated to continually poke their 17-year-old children in the side so that the kids will stay awake in our meetings. Wouldn't you hope that, by the time a child is a senior in high school, she could be responsible for regulating her own sleep cycle?)

Whoever said, "Kids learn from overcoming failure, not from avoiding failure" got it right. In 2013, we need to communicate to our children that their world is basically a safe place, that—for now at least—there are enough mastodon burgers to go around.

79

In order to bring up healthy kids in this tough culture, it's important to know whom to trust. Anyone who claims to know—unequivocally—what is in your child's interest should be met with a great deal of skepticism.

Position Open: All Powerful Wizard of Oz

Did you, by any chance, buy Qualcomm for two dollars a share in 1992? If you were that prescient, did you sell all your Qualcomm holdings eight years later for $75 a share? Because had you invested ten thousand dollars at the start of the run-up, you would have walked out of the casino with $375K. In eight years, each dollar you invested would have turned into $37.50.

Similarly, did you short Qualcomm (make a bet that the price of the stock would go down) in 2000? If you had, within 18 months your money would have gone up by a factor of 1000 as the stock price plummeted like a flying sheep.* As Qualcomm lost over 90 percent of its value, there is almost no limit to the amount of money you could have made by wagering that its price would go down.

A college admissions counselor in a high school in New York told a student that she should "under no circumstances" bother applying to Brandeis University because the student "had no chance of being admitted." A college admissions counselor in Florida told a student not to study photography, that the student would be better off studying accounting. "There are no jobs in photography," the counselor pontificated. "All the newspapers are going under. There will always be jobs for accountants."

Ignoring for a moment the absurdity of the counselor's underlying assumptions—that the purpose of college is to get a job; that a student who loves photography COULD change to accounting at the drop of a hat; that the counselor is able to make accurate long-term prognostications about the job market—can we address the virulent and strident agenda of "I know better than you"?

Because at some level, that's what this is really about: I'm older, I know better, and I know what's best for you.

Does this counselors have the wrong sign on her office door? Rather than "Amanda B. Recondwith, College Counselor," should her nameplate read, "Mandy R., College Counselor and All Powerful Wizard of Oz"?

Because someone who can predict where the jobs will be in four years should be making stock picks or sending girls back to Kansas in a balloon rather than working in a college advising office.

Is there some possibility that a 17-year-old should have the agency and ability to make some decisions for herself? Haven't good students earned the right to make some guesses, take some steps in the direction of self-determination?

I'm not talking about kids who have decided that drinking wine in the gutter is their life plan. Suicidal kids, kids who self-harm, kids who commit crimes, and kids who sell drugs all need to be redirected to paths that will allow them to grow up.

But kids who have done well in school, who have made reasonable choices have earned the right to take a step—even a misstep—in the direction of determining their own destiny.

Because, if you think about it, even the Wizard of Oz only gives gentle guidance and advice. After the blustering and pontificating is over, he helps out rather than takes control. And for all we know, the Scarecrow's diploma says Bachelors of Arts in Photography, not Bachelors of Business in Accounting.

In short, loving parents and competent counselors should model, instruct, and guide. That's why the plaque on our door reads GUIDE-ance COUNSELOR. There are no words to the effect of ALL POWERFUL.

Unless, of course, you bought Qualcomm in 1992 and sold it in 2000. In that case—and in that case only—you can unequivocally tell my child where she'll be admitted to college and what to study when she gets there.

* "Notice they do not so much fly as plummet."
                    —Monty Python, Flying Sheep Skit, 1969

The greatest gift we can give to our high school seniors is the understanding that it's not where they get admitted to college that matters, but what they can do once they get there.

Pow! Smack! Oof!

Envision vicious combatants locked in a zero-sum game in which only a small number can survive and only one can triumph. Imagine the contestants scratching, clawing, and punching one another for any and every competitive advantage. "*Omnes contra omnes*" wrote Hobbes. "All against all." No quarter asked or given. Winner take all and devil take the hindmost.

Is my topic this week mixed martial arts? Or am I writing about *The Hunger Games*? Am I describing your first marriage and subsequent litigious divorce?

Nah. Of course, I'm writing about admissions to competitive colleges.

On Sunday, you tell your children to love their neighbors. Every religious tradition has a similar version of Deuteronomy 19:18. But on Monday, our kids get a different message: if you help your classmate study for her chemistry exam, she will get a better grade; she will be graduated closer to the top of the class; she will get the last scholarship; she will be the one to absorb the scarce resources. She will be admitted to a TOP COLLEGE. And you won't!

Indeed, rather than being admitted to a top college, if your child gives of herself and helps her neighbor study, your child will end up drinking wine in the gutter. She won't be admitted to a top college. If she helps her classmate, she may not go to college at all! Excellent chemistry student that she is, she will still fail at everything forever more!

If the paradigm is "there is only one cabbage and I want MY daughter to have that cabbage," then it could be argued that your daughter won't have any cabbage. But the counterintuitive and very good news is that in college admissions, there are more than enough metaphorical cabbages to go around. Indeed, some college cabbages aren't even harvested and rot, uneaten.

The vast majority of colleges admit virtually every qualified applicant. The issue isn't "Where can you get in?" but "What can you DO in the classroom once you are admitted?" Your valedictorian president-of-the-school daughter with perfect SAT scores was denied at Princeton? Your valedictorian president-of-the-school daughter with perfect SAT scores has to go to Franklin and Marshall instead?

Oh, the horror!

Last I checked there were a great many successful, content professionals who had called Lancaster home for four years. If those students were competent IN the classroom at F&M, they did just fine subsequently.

It will come as no surprise that many of my clients applying to competitive colleges are writhing shells of stressed out, lonely kids for whom high school is a miserable series of solitary vigils and anxiety-ridden evaluations. Are these wraiths reading and learning until the wee hours because the books and ideas are the most cogent in the history of civilization? Are they doing projects and writing papers because they are fascinated by Sophocles, Newton, Shakespeare, and Virginia Wolfe? Not so much. These automatons

278

are learning for the sake of grades, grades, and more grades. They are learning for the sake of class rank. They are learning for the sake of admissions to competitive colleges.

What's the way to win this game? Is it possible to "stack the deck," to ensure that your daughter wins and that everyone else's daughter loses? Is there a "fix" so that your valedictorian son with an 800 on his math SAT is admitted and everyone else's valedictorian son with 800 on his math SAT is denied?

Nope.

Beyond a point, admissions to hyper-competitive colleges is random. Arbitrary. A roll of the dice. Based on factors beyond the control of the student. Is a beautiful sunset better than a strawberry milkshake? Depends how thirsty you are. Is that tuba player from the small town in the Midwest "better" than that yearbook editor from that major metropolitan area? Unless you're willing to move to Kenosha and hand your child a tuba, the answer may not matter.

The other possible solution to the issue of competitive college admissions is as straight-forward as it is effective: don't buy a ticket for that train.

Rather than insisting your kids compete in a sick game where the best-case scenario is that they crawl to the top over the lifeless bodies of their shattered fellow students, suggest instead that they learn to collaborate. Help them learn to cooperate, to give a classmate a hand.

Our world will be a better place and your children will benefit if you allow them to "do unto others" each and every day of the week. And because they are not only accomplished students but also good citizens, they'll do even better—even if they happen to be denied at a top college.

81

What gifts can loving parents give their children when they have gone seriously off-track?

Tommy, Can You Hear Me? (Part One)

"It's all your fault, Mom. You are the reason I don't have any friends. All of the other kids drive nice cars, but you gave me this lousy car to drive. The other kids make fun of me. If you would just leave me alone, everything would be okay."

"But, Honey, if I leave you alone, you don't even get up and go to school never mind do your homework. You just stay in your room playing that video game until one in the morning."

"See, there you go again. Always badgering me. Don't you see how this is all your fault?"

"No, I don't see how it's all my fault at all. Your father and I work hard to provide for you and your brothers."

"There you go again. Always comparing me to my brothers who are so perfect. 'Why can't you get good grades like your brothers? Why can't you help out around the house like your brothers?' It's always the same thing. Why can't you just leave me alone?"

"We try to leave you alone, but you keep getting suspended from school and arrested."

"Why can't you just shut up, you stupid wench? I told you that wasn't my fault."

"It wasn't your fault that you had marijuana in your book bag?"

"No, it wasn't. How many times do I have to explain it to you? The pot wasn't mine. Somebody must have put the dope in my book bag."

"Anyway, what time do you want me to pick you up after school today?"

"I don't want you to pick me up from school today at all. I hope you die."

Fast forward a year from the conversation transcribed above and edited for a family publication—Tommy didn't actually use the word "wench." Tommy has been graduated from high school—barely—but has been kicked out of his college dorm for smoking marijuana. His midterm grades were two Cs, a D, and an F. He has stopped going to one of his classes and has not turned in assignments in two of the others.

"Tommy, what are we going to do?"

"I told you: I'm going to get a job. Next semester I'll go back to school."

"But you don't ever go out looking for work. All you do is play on your computer."

"You are so stupid. That's how it is nowadays, Mom. All the jobs are online."

"We only want what is best for you. Your father and I are only trying to help."

"That's it. You keep bothering me. Why can't you ever just shut up? I can't stand this anymore. I'm out of here."

And Tommy takes off. He has ten thousand dollars in his own name, an inheritance from his grandfather's brother who died when Tommy was a boy. Not surprisingly, within six weeks, the money is almost gone, having disappeared in a cloud of pot smoke, an orgy of video gaming, motel bills, and tak-out pizza.

At eleven o'clock at night, Tommy's mother answers her cell phone.

"Mom, it's me, your son."

"Are you okay? We haven't heard from you. We've been so worried."

"I'm fine. Listen, I need money."

"Tommy, your father and I have decided not to give you any money. You need treatment. We'll pay for you to get help, but we won't pay for you to smoke pot, play video games, and live in a motel."

"That's crazy. There's nothing wrong with me. You and dad are the ones with the problem. I just need a few dollars to see me through for a little bit. I'm going to get a job. And I don't smoke pot. Who told you I smoke pot? This is all your fault. I'm your son. If you love me, you'll give me some money. You've never cared for me; you only love my brothers. You have enough money. Give me some money or I'll be living on the street. Do you want me to be homeless? Is that what you want?"

What should Tommy's mother say?

Should she send Tommy some money? Should she allow Tommy to move back home? Should she insist that Tommy go to a program to get help for his addiction to marijuana?

What if Tommy refuses to go to a program? What if he does decide to live "at the corner of 'WALK' and 'DON'T WALK'"? What should Tommy's mother do?

82

Families Anonymous* has many insightful signs. My favorite reads, "You didn't cause it; you can't control it; you can't cure it." Sometimes even the most loving families can't make the situation any better, but they can avoid making it worse.

Tommy, Can You Hear Me? (Part Two: Insights and Answers)

"I've changed, Mom. I'm not going to smoke pot any more or play video games either. I just need some money until I can get a job." Tommy pauses as if for dramatic effect then plays the card that has always worked in the past: "I can't believe you don't trust me."

How should Tommy's mom respond?

Should she explain that trust is a bucket that gets emptied all at once, but is filled up one drop at a time?

284

Should she articulate that Tommy has failed to achieve his purpose repeatedly and that unless he gets treatment no further communication will be forthcoming except of course that she will stay on the phone just this one last time to say the same things that she's said six bazillion times before and that maybe just maybe this time will be the time that her cogent pleas connect and Tommy agrees to treatment?

(Nah, that can't be the right answer. The correct choice is never a run-on sentence.)

It's time for Tommy's mom to COMMUNICATE that there is no more discussion. Either Tommy accepts the gift of treatment or he doesn't. There is nothing else to discuss.

Tommy's mom doesn't have to say, "No, we're not going to send you any money;" she doesn't have to say, "You can't live at home again;" she doesn't have to say, "Marijuana and a video game addiction are destroying you." She doesn't have to say anything.

The time for talk is past. Now is time for action. And actions, as has often been remarked, speak louder than words.

As long as Tommy's mom is still TALKING, Tommy has every reason to believe that the old dance will continue: Tommy will be abusive. Mom will be patient. Tommy will argue irrationally about the past. Mom will be conciliatory. Tommy will turn up the heat on guilt. Mom will fold.

And as Skinner taught us, a differential reinforcement schedule takes the longest to extinguish.**

There comes a point after you've validated the feeling that your child truly wants a pony, there comes a point after you've mentioned that in your apartment building residents are not allowed to have a pony, there comes a point where subsequent discussion on the subject of pony acquisition becomes superfluous.

Marshall McLuhan said "the medium is the message." For Tommy, the message needs to be a dial tone. Tommy's mom has to hang up the phone and not take any more calls, texts, emails, or smoke signals from her son. Either he agrees to treatment or there is nothing else to talk about.

Tommy doesn't have to agree with mom's cogent point that he does indeed need treatment. Tommy doesn't have to look forward to treatment. Tommy doesn't have to agree to the goal of treatment.

He just has to go.

"But he'll starve, he'll be homeless, he'll come to harm," every loving parent cries. Maybe so. But if he comes home or Mom sends money, Tommy's mom might as well just buy him the pot that he's going to continue smoking every day.

"But shouldn't we address his learning differences, his self-esteem issues, the reasons he's self-medicating?" No. All these issues have been addressed repeatedly and to no avail.

"But shouldn't we send him to a therapist?" No. You and I both know that Tommy has seen every competent therapist in town since the time he turned nine.

Families Anonymous has signs: "You didn't cause it; you can't control it; you can't cure it." It's time for Tommy's mom to hold the line: get treatment.

Or you're on your own.

*Typically a great group and there's a meeting near you!

**A pigeon is taught that she will receive a food pellet when she pushes a bar. Subsequently, if the food stops, the pigeon will soon stop pushing the bar. But if the pellets arrive sporadically—every seventh push or every ninth push—the pigeon will keep pushing the bar pretty much indefinitely.

83

Before our children commit to devoting ten thousand hours to achieve proficiency in a discipline, doesn't it behoove loving parents to ensure, to the best of our ability, that the child matches the subject? Can you imagine studying something you didn't like for ten thousand hours?

Coulda, Shoulda, Woulda

Much is made of Malcolm Gladwell's thoughtful insight that to achieve proficiency, the equivalent of five years of full time work is a necessary requirement—if not a sufficient one. The Beatles played clubs in Hambourg for ten thousand hours before appearing on The Ed Sullivan Show; Steve Jobs futzed around with computers for ten thousand hours before moving on to enforce his prodigious ability worldwide.

What isn't mentioned is how many people put in the requisite ten thousand hours and achieve competence but not success. My buddy, Kevin, played guitar for ten thousand hours and didn't make it to a German Coffee House never mind CBS. There is something to be said, certainly, for how beautifully he plays. Here's another question: what else could he have done with his time?

One of my clients tells his children that each decision closes doors. "If you drop math, there are a number of jobs that you can't have," he cautions. "A career in actuarial science is not an option if you don't take advanced math courses." Point taken.

But kids who drop math are frequently those who CAN'T go on to a more advanced course, not those who REFUSE to keep plugging along with the curriculum. If Percival has the ABILITY to take second-semester calculus, then by all means, I encourage Percy to learn the integral of one over x. But if he's destined to suffer unnecessarily before getting a miserable D in Calc II, let's allow him to study that at which he might excel.

Don't misunderstand: I'm pleased to be fluent in trigonometry. There's not much I enjoy more than showing a promising student an identity or solving a novel problem. But I wonder what else might have been written on the hard drive of my brain. COULD I have learned to speak fluent Russian in the time I invested studying sines and angles? Could my neurons have been put to different use?

Look back over your choices, those of my gentle readers who are old enough to remember where the two roads diverged in the yellow wood of your past. What might you have done had you felt all the paths were yours to explore?

Running 50 miles in Nashville a few weeks ago was 11 hours and 13 minutes spent away from other pleasures—playing guitar, for example, or working on my archery. (Not that Eric Clapton has anything to worry about, mind you. And no, I don't actually know a bow and arrow from a bow-tie.)

When we force—or attempt to force—our children to try to excel in those areas in which they have little aptitude or affection, we not only suggest that they bang their heads against the wall but we also forbid them the opportunity to learn those disciplines that they might enjoy and in which they might excel.

Obviously, we want our kids to have functional abilities in reading, writing, and arithmetic. But beyond a certain level, don't you sometimes feel that the advanced courses are too—for want of a better word—"advanced?"

After all, most people are able to muddle through life without knowing a whole heckuvalot about logarithms. I don't remember Ed Sullivan asking John Lennon to solve any equations. Or as a brilliant student is alleged to have cheerfully written on an exam that asked her to "find x" in a drawing of a triangle, "There it is!"

As Gilbert and Sullivan's Modern Major General put it:

I'm very well acquainted, too, with matters mathematical,
I understand equations both the simple and quadratical
About the binomial theorem I am teaming with a lot o' news
With many cheerful facts about the square of the hypotenuse.

The joke in the *Pirates of Penzance* is that the MMG might do well to have some military knowledge as well.

All learning—math, language, poetry, history, medicine, mechanics, athletics, survival, geography, music— is worthwhile and at least a cursory knowledge of each is worthwhile. Competence cannot be exaggerated. But with such a limited number of ten thousand hours to invest as we strut and fret our hour upon the stage, we have to think carefully about our choices. Because as wonderful as it is to know all there is to know about trigonometry, there's something to be said for being able to speak Russian, rebuild an engine, hit a fastball, and being...

"… very good at integral and differential calculus;
[and knowing] the scientific names of beings animalculous."

84

Before making fun of the speaker of this parody of good parenting, it would be wise to make sure that we aren't making the same mistakes on a smaller level ourselves. Do we want what is best for our children for them—or for ourselves?

Here Comes the Sun

Having carefully studied the pH levels of the dirt, I dug a garden plot in the yard with full sun and proper drainage. Having prepared the soil with the appropriate levels of fertilizer, I planted seeds according to the almanac, waiting for the most propitious day.

The seed package said the seeds would germinate in eight days. You can understand, therefore, how frustrated I was when it turned out that my seedlings didn't start to show up until ten or 11 days after I had planted them. I want to give my plants every advantage, so I added more fertilizer even though the "experts" said to wait, that too much fertilizer could be harmful.

"Experts!" Hah! If some fertilizer is good, then more fertilizer must be better. It stands to reason.

But my plants still weren't doing well—obviously there was something wrong with the soil—so I took the next logical step: I dug them up and carefully transplanted them to a sunnier spot with even better drainage. Of course I was meticulous in ensuring that the fragile root structures weren't damaged. I'm not an idiot; I know how tender seedlings are at that age.

But for reasons that no one could possibly begin to explain—and believe me, I asked everyone who would listen—the plants did even worse in their new location. Clearly, they weren't getting enough sun. There is no other possible explanation that fits all the facts. My neighbor's plants were now doing significantly better than mine. He hadn't done anything to help his plants grow. He just waters a few times a week and does some occasional weeding.

That bastard!

He must be singing to his plants or having his plants listen to "Seedling Einstein." (Of course it's too late now for me, but I'm pretty certain I should have had my seeds listen to Mozart before they sprouted.) And I'm sure that "Seedling Einstein" is helpful. It costs so much that it must be worthwhile.

Although it's too late now. My plants are way behind. They're wilted and weak. Their stems aren't strong and their leaves are droopy. Maybe I was wrong to transplant them when they were so little, but I take comfort in the fact that I made the best decisions I could with the information that I had and with love in my heart. All I want is for my plants to be bigger and healthier than those of my neighbor. Is that too much to ask? I just want my tomatoes to be bigger, healthier, and tastier than his.

Fortunately, I have an idea. This one I know will work. Sunshine is good for plants. If a little sunshine is good, then a lot of sunshine must be better. It must be. Therefore, I've taken my remaining funds and have purchased several dozen little magnifying glasses. I'm going to set up each magnifying glass to focus the light of the sun on each of my surviving seedlings. (Yes, many of my plants have died. But that was their fault. They didn't try hard enough; they didn't care as much as they needed to; they CHOSE not to grow and learn in spite of all I did for them, after all the sacrifices I made.)

Don't tell me that there's nothing more I can do. Don't tell me that I can't have a bigger, better, tastier tomato than my neighbor. And for God's sake, don't tell me that I can't make the situation better, only worse. Don't tell me that I should get a life. All I've ever wanted is a better tomato than that of my neighbor. Is that so wrong?

***

At the risk of "explaining the joke," here is why the speaker above should not be issued a fishing license let alone be allowed anywhere near a developing child. Er, ahem. Of course, I meant a growing "plant."

Here are the analogous bad ideas:

1) Planning a pregnancy based on when the child will start school so that the child will be the biggest or the smartest. A better plan is to help the child fit in where she is. If she's the smartest or the dumbest or the tallest or the shortest or the most social or the least social, she needs to be comfortable in her own skin. She needs to be loved and valued for who she is, not for what she does. (And don't even get me started on mothers who "red shirt" their kindergarten sons so that the boys can be a year older and a year bigger when they play football as high school seniors.)

2) Too much fertilizer IS a bad idea. So is too much sunlight. Reading *Fox in Socks* to a six-year-old at bed time is loving. Reading *War and Peace* to a six-year-old is abusive.

3) Obsessing on how the child is doing every minute says more about the anxiety of the parent than about the health of the child. Kids make mistakes; that's how they learn. Uprooting them, making snap changes, becoming hysterical are all iatrogenic. (That is, cause harm by trying to help.)

Most importantly: in raising healthy kids, the only way to "win" is not to compete. Every child is a gift. Not just the one who is graduated first in her class.

Every healthy tomato is wonderful.

292

Notes

Made in the USA
San Bernardino, CA
02 December 2013